the e-factor

the e-factor

Building a 24/7, Customer-Centric, Electronic Business for the Internet Age

Martin T. Focazio

AMACOM
American Management Association
New York • Atlanta • Boston • Chicago • Kansas City • San Francisco • Washington, D.C.
Brussels • Mexico City • Tokyo • Toronto

Special discounts on bulk quantities of AMACOM books are
available to corporations, professional associations, and other
organizations. For details, contact Special Sales Department,
AMACOM, a division of American Management Association,
1601 Broadway, New York, NY 10019.
Tel.: 212-903-8316. Fax: 212-903-8083.
Web Site: www. amacombooks.org

This publication is designed to provide accurate and authoritative
information in regard to the subject matter covered. It is sold with
the understanding that the publisher is not engaged in rendering
legal, accounting, or other professional service. If legal advice or other
expert assistance is required, the services of a competent professional
person should be sought.

Library of Congress Cataloging-in-Publication Data

Focazio, Martin T., 1965-
    The E-Factor : building a 24/7 customer-centric, electronic business for the
    Internet age / Martin T. Focazio.
       p. cm.
    Includes index.
    ISBN 0-8144-0489-8
    1. Electronic commerce. 1. Title.

HF5548.32 .F63 2001
658.8'4—dc21

                                                                        00-045117

Printing number

10 9 8 7 6 5 4 3 2 1

CONTENTS

the e-factor

INTRODUCTION

You have a really cool Web site, one with pretty graphics and maybe a Java applet scrolling text across the screen. The more high tech the better, right? Sure, but what does this site do for your customers? What about the bottom line? And how do you plan to operate the site on a daily basis?

This book will guide you through the maze that is e-commerce. I don't mean how to create a

Web site—electronic commerce is more than fancy Web servers, good visual design, and online shopping. I'm talking about how to strategically incorporate e-commerce and the reality of an electronic world into your daily business. E-commerce is about forming and managing effective interactive relationships with your target audiences. Managers must incorporate a Web site that is more than just about the company. It *is* the company. This book will help you understand how the interactive world affects your business plan and how to plan to manage an organization that is always open for business.

Over the course of the next couple hundred pages, I'll introduce key concepts of interactive business development and coordinate those concepts with a sequence of projects and deliverables that will lead your company to a rational approach to developing your online presence. Specifically, when you finish this book you should be able to:

- Identify your business "type" from the five presented
- Identify goals and form a flexible action plan to attain those goals through the application of interactive communications
- Identify the right set of audiences for your interactive services
- Work around a corporate culture that is resistant to online media

- Create an information routing structure
- Implement an effective interactive service
- Maintain and continually improve your interactive service
- Monitor the return on investment (ROI) of your electronic efforts

Once, a long time ago in the 1970s, most retail stores remained closed on Sunday. Gradually, as antiquated laws were repealed or ignored, some stores began to open on Sunday. At first, most stores chose to stay closed, but in time they found that in order to compete with those stores that were open on Sunday, they too were forced to be open. For many stores, it was not a profitable day of the week, but the competitive landscape required a Sunday opening in order to meet customer expectations. As anyone who has been to a Home Depot store on a Sunday will attest, things have changed, and Sunday is a vital selling day to retailers.

For some companies, it seems that the decision to become an e-business or not is like the decision facing those retailers back in the 1970s. Right now there don't appear to be too many customers. Most business happens "during the week" (in traditional modes), and it costs a lot of money to open up the business on "Sunday."

Think of doing business online as having an eighth day of the week—call it "e-day." E-day is the day that all businesses are open, even at two in the morning. E-day is the day that the salesperson is in. E-day is the day customers can go shopping because they are not at work. E-day is the day that is most convenient for the customer to do business.

Your business can choose to be open on e-day or not, but if you choose not to be open, remember that there are plenty of hungry companies looking for new opportunities to do business with your customers on e-day—and your competitors will find your best customers.

1

THE ELECTRONIC ECONOMY

■■■■ What the Heck Is Going on Here?

Dot-com . . . bricks and mortar . . . clicks and mortar. . . it seems like the Internet is radically affecting traditional businesses and creating a vast new economy, one of companies without profits, businesses with no discernable revenue models and staggering market valuations. The

Internet has seemingly disrupted the standard way of running a profitable business. But it hasn't, actually.

The Internet *itself* is not causing this disruption. The *use* of the Internet to do business in a way that avoids additional costs, reduces current costs, and facilitates massive one-to-one communication is the driver of the new economy.

If you've picked up this book, you're probably wondering where the Internet is going to take your business over the next few years. I can't begin to answer that question for you here. What I can do is identify how you can change your thinking about how business is done to adapt to an electronic economy. This book is all about figuring out what to do first to ensure that your company both survives and thrives with the help of interactive communications and the Internet.

In this new economy there is a new way for a company or a brand to deliver value. To borrow a concept from Nicolas Negroponte, the noted author of *Being Digital* and a founding investor in *Wired* magazine, the primary value of the new economic success story is in the "bits" (that is, digital information), not in the "atoms" (that is, physical objects). A company can deliver value to the customer as bits through either interactive technologies, such as the Web or e-mail, or physical objects, such as retail outlets or catalogs.

Investors intuitively recognize that the value of the bits can often exceed that of the atoms, and thus the market valuations of companies like Yahoo! exceed their physical assets by an exponential factor. The bit-based company interacts with a customer in a new way. It is able to supply customers with what they want at the moment they have a need, whereas customers of atom-based companies must instead use a physical presence to fulfill a need (for example, go to the mall). The company that realizes that interactive technology unlocks the value in the bits will succeed. It will do so whether bits are used for better and lower-cost customer service, revenue generation from intellectual property, effective distribution of knowledge capital, or simply a more effective decision support system for a presales activity.

Interactive technologies are not just limited to Web sites and e-mail. Those are just "training wheels" for the next phase of the new economy. Wireless, ubiquitous access through a multitude of devices is already happening and will be an important part of the economy in less than three years. For example, the Palm Pilot VII, made by Palm Computing, has wireless e-mail and simple Internet access technologies and is a precursor to the portable, mobile consumer information appliance that will be as common as the television set is today. In Japan, the DoComO service, a simple and fast wireless data service, is the hottest thing for teens. They use their wireless devices to send one another notes or music and to play games. These teens are growing up fast, and they will expect to do business with these devices soon.

Companies that develop or extend their value with bits, that is, adjust their philosophies to match an electronic economy, will be positioned to succeed as new technologies are introduced and popularized.

It Is a "Bit" More Complicated Than You Might Expect

Using bits to define or enhance your value as an organization means much more than creating a compelling Web site. Doing business with inter-active technology is fundamentally different from doing so with established models. The dif-ference involves more than just selling direct from a factory to the end user over the Internet, as Dell Computer does, or having a business model in which you sell things for less than you paid for them, as is done with Buy.com. Doing business with interactive technologies is all about clarifying the "fog of battle" so common in business. It means that when a customer buys something online, accounting knows about it, the ledgers are updated, and inventory is adjust-ed. It means that when merchandise is shipped, the customer, the warehouse, and the salesperson all know about the shipment simultaneously. But all this activity leads to the most basic concept of doing business with interactive technologies—establishing a boundary-free marketplace with multiple sales channels.

Multiple Sales Channels

Many traditional companies sell goods and services through multiple channels such as retail outlets, catalogs, and direct sales. For the most part, these multiple channels avoid conflicting with one another. By dividing sales territories physically or changing pricing structures among channels, conflict is usually avoided. With online businesses, there are no physical territorial divisions, and it doesn't take a genius to find the true price of an item. This setup and capability have forced companies to look at the world in a different way. Hard questions such as "do we support our channels, destroy them, or is there another way?" must now be answered. You can't postpone this issue, and you can't deny how important it is.

Toys 'R' Us is one company struggling with sales channel issues in its bid to dominate toy sales. The toy company was a late entrant to the e-commerce arena. After losing their number-one ranking for toy sales to Wal-Mart during the 1998 Christmas season, Toys 'R' Us decided to make a go at Web-based sales. However, their first choice for an executive to head up the online sales offering backed out quickly, citing Toys 'R' Us's lack of commitment to a site that would compete on price head-to-head with their own retail operations. Retail store managers had protested vigorously against lower prices in the online store, afraid that the lower online store prices would cannibalize retail sales. But the lower prices were necessary to compete more effectively against leading start-ups such as eToys.com and SmarterKids.com. They forged an agreement with a venture capital company, Benchmark Capital, which was enlisted not only to infuse capital but also to provide e-commerce expertise. That agreement also crumbled because of Toys 'R' Us's unwillingness to give up control over the operation.[1] Eventually, the toy company went at it alone and experienced a disastrous Christmas 1999 season. A lack of good internal processes and technical infrastructure forced the company to notify customers on December 21, 1999, that they would *not* be getting their orders in time for Christmas, some of which had been placed as far back as Thanksgiving! Instead, the company gave customers 100 "Geoffrey Bucks" to use at the stores to appease them. Toys 'R' Us's lack of full commitment to an Internet strategy, as well as their lack of willingness to accept that the rules of e-commerce are different from the rules by which they have always played, did serious damage to the company's brand value and reputation. Ultimately, the Geoffrey Bucks did nothing to solve the dilemma. By the summer of 2000, Toys 'R' Us gave up trying to run their own e-commerce operation and formed a partnership with Amazon.com.

Any company grappling with channel conflict when attempting an online commerce initiative is facing a hard reality: A carefully crafted and managed distribution channel may be a business liability in the long term but is utterly necessary in the short term. In the end, you must decide if short-term pain is worth long-term gains as the market shifts to a new way of doing business.

Disruptive Technologies

In many cases, the core business model upon which an organization is built is shattered by the capabilities of the Internet. Clayton Christenson describes this disruption in his powerful book, *The Innovator's Dilemma*.[2] He points out that even well-managed companies that listen to their customers and invest in new technologies can lose market dominance. "Disruptive" technologies are often overlooked by market leaders because of their appeal to the lower end of the market or because the revenue potential does not seem to be significant. Market leaders often do not see the value in competing in this low-end developing segment, often fearing that they will cannibalize their current sales or destroy their image, until their business has been overrun by competitors. Only those companies that are willing in effect to "steal" their own markets will be able to hang onto market share.

Many examples of this type of conflict exist, but one of the best can be found in the retail brokerage industry, which for decades was a closed "club" with limited membership. In 1990, it was virtually impossible for an individual to buy a stock without a broker. Now, 25 percent of all stocks are traded online, and 60 percent of American households own stock.[3] In the summer of 1999, Merrill Lynch, after several years of insisting that it would not "give in" to online trading, announced that it too would introduce low-cost online trading. Their broker-based core structure was feeling the pressure on price structures. While Merrill Lynch was charging hundreds of dollars for a trade, low-cost online competitors were offering trades for a flat fee as low as $8.95. In addition, an increasingly educated public was actually *wanting* to make self-directed investment decisions, discounting the value Merrill Lynch's full-service brokers could bring to the table. This development forced a complete rethinking of how Merrill Lynch would do business in the future. But the launch didn't come without pain. Broker commissions have been declining, and other brokerage houses are recruiting the top performers. It is still too early to say whether or not Merrill Lynch will be able to weather the storm in the long run, but assets are up 20 percent, indicating that the company has been able to stem the tide of the defections to competing online services.[4]

■ Core Concepts of the Electronic Economy

In an effort to resolve issues that occur as a result of the electronic economy, many businesses look to success stories of the Internet, such as FedEx, Dell, Yahoo!, and Cisco. They seek to learn how these companies built themselves up into online powerhouses and hope to leverage that knowledge for their own businesses. Unfortunately, looking at historical success stories typically has little or no bearing on current business strategy issues, because the technology simply moves too quickly. One of the most shocking and difficult things for a manager to realize is that in this new marketplace, studying "best practices" of the way business *used* to be done as little as a year ago is not the way to learn how to succeed online today. Competitive advantage is now measured in weeks and months, not quarters and years.

Things can change so quickly. For example, a small company called Hotmail created a Web-based e-mail system. At the time of its creation, it was not a unique idea. There were other Web-based e-mail systems in use. But Hotmail had the idea to append a small, two-line marketing message to each e-mail sent through the Hotmail services. This was the "magic bullet" that made Hotmail take off. Every message sent by Hotmail users carried a marketing message.

The service grew quickly, and in less than two years it was purchased by Microsoft—for $450 million! Soon after, Web-based e-mail services became commonplace. What was once a high-value competitive advantage was quickly reduced to a commodity expectation. Now Web-based e-mail is common on sites such as CNN, iVillage, and just about any other major Web property. Web-based e-mail as a strategic advantage had about a four-month lifespan.

How do you realize strategic advantage in the interactive space? Look to the core concepts of the electronic economy. Here they are in five points:

1. The point of promise is the point of proof
2. The customer is the center of the universe
3. Infostructure is more important than infrastructure
4. Your biggest competitor is not who you think it is
5. The future is not what it used to be

The Point of Promise Is the Point of Proof

In any business relationship, it is possible to divide the customer experience into two simple parts: the point of *promise* and the point of *proof.*

At the simplest level, the point of promise is any aspect of a business relationship in which the customer or potential customer is presented with a branding message, an offer, a call to action, or a value proposition. A point of promise is when your company does any of the following:

- Builds "top-of-mind" awareness
- Asserts the value of the brand
- Makes claims to prove the value of the brand
- Offers a value proposition to the customer
- Proposes a transaction of information or financial exchange

Points of promise can be any of the following:

- Advertisements in mass media (television, newspaper, opt-in e-mail, etc.)
- Sponsorships
- In-store experiences
- Web sites

The second part of the business relationship is

the point of proof. This is the point at which business is done. The point of proof is found any time a customer actually takes action to accept the offer. The point of proof is when the customer can do any of the following:

- Conduct business with your company
- Follow through on your call to action
- Experience the value of the brand
- Test and prove your company's claims
- Communicate with the right party
- Obtain relevant decision support
- Transact value (in the form of money or information) with your company

In a traditional business, various hurdles arise between the point of promise and the point of proof. Your customer must make an effort to go from a point of promise to a point of proof. Examples of such hurdles might include:

- The need to travel to a particular location for proof (the mall, the store, etc.)
- The need to make a phone call and navigate endless, useless company-centric voicemail mazes ('Press 1 for sales, press 2 for parts, press 3 for . . .")
- The customer's time frame

Of course, these are just examples. A customer may have to leap over many other types of hurdles to actually do business with your company. With each hurdle, you risk having the customer lose interest in the relationship.

Interactive communication eliminates the hurdles. The real power of interactive communications lies in the fact that from the customer's perspective, there are no hurdles between the point of promise and the point of proof. The point of promise *is* the point of proof.

Think about this scenario: customers responding to an offer immediately—using your information technology to link with your company directly. There is no need for the customer to switch tools, change communication modes, or change behavior to respond to a company's promise or value proposition. This scenario is not only possible in today's economy of interactive communications, it is becoming almost commonplace. Customers are now expecting to be empowered to do business at the moment they are engaged. If your company can't meet this expectation, you stand to lose a segment of your market.

Let's explore two examples of this concept in action. On the Dell Computer home page at www.dell.com the customer sees a wide variety of engaging value propositions, with the offer to

"Buy a Great Computer Direct from Dell" prominently displayed. In the traditional world of communications, the customer would have to remember the offer and utilize another communications tool to get to the point of proof. The customer might have to call or write or visit a store to be able to get to the point of proof.

In the interactive communications model, because the point of promise and the point of proof are one and the same, the customer can go to the next logical step—to begin the process of buying a Dell computer—with minimum effort and maximum value. One mouse click will take the customer to the "store."

For the online audience, being empowered is not just about having the ability to buy products. Online companies can provide other money-making services. For example, eBay, the online auction service, allows its customers to harness the power of interactive communications to *sell* online as well. The eBay home screen incorporates a number of value propositions to both buyers and sellers, such as the range of categories and the number of page views a month. In this context, the promise of the audience can lead to customers adding an auction to the eBay database to leverage a much larger audience than they could find on their own. Maybe a customer can sell that Joe DiMaggio rookie card he suspected was worth something all along.

The Customer Is the Center of the Universe

Every business pundit out there has been telling you for decades that you need to be customer-focused. So what's changed in the electronic economy? Customers' expectations and their ability to change allegiances.

Customers have experiences outside of the simple exchange of goods. Customer service, quality of goods, and many other factors influence customer perception. The online environment has expanded their expectations. Your customers are now comparing their experience at Amazon.com to their online experience with your company. For example, Amazon.com sends confirmation e-mails moments after an order is placed. Although this effort is technically trivial, it signals the customer that the company is "open" all the time.

Online communications technologies have provided customers with the ability to obtain on-demand customer services through new communications channels that provide nearly instant response. They can get rapid price comparisons across vendors, bid/ask data for goods and services, and buy or sell in a global marketplace. New companies not bound by traditional channels and infrastructure are training your customers to expect exceptionally fast, completely authoritative, and accurate information through interactive communications channels. Can your company provide that?

The customer expects a seamless operation. Before the Internet became popular, 70 percent of the work a company did was invisible to its customers. So many back-office processes, from product development to accounting, are traditionally hidden from view by stores or a sales force. However, the real power (and challenge) of e-business is letting the customers interact with the "real" company directly. This means thinking of each and every Internet-connected computer as a workstation connected to your internal systems.

Many companies, unfortunately, are imposing the physical structure of their organization on the electronic organization. How many times have you seen "splash screens," those screens with a great logo that require you to "click to enter" the company rather than giving you quick and easy access to information? Or how many corporate Web sites have subdirectories based on areas of the company, such as sales, manufacturing, or investor relations? Customers don't care about these divisions of labor. In fact, these Web sites create needless hurdles for the customer to jump. The Dell Computer Web site is, again, an excellent example of a customer-centric Web site. The company includes categories based on customer needs: Home Computers, Small Offices, Enterprise Servers, Government Buyer, Education, Health Care.

If you organize the Web site by customer need, how do you meld the distinct areas of the company (for example, sales, operations, and technology) that hold a stake in the information? Bringing the points of promise and proof together requires interaction among these groups. The sales and marketing department can't make a promise and then rely on operations to fulfill it. The promise and the proof must be offered up simultaneously or the customer, who expects a seamless experience, will go elsewhere; and it won't be difficult to move on if your competitor has set up a customer-centric operation.

The result of all this "exposure" of internal process via the Internet is that it is increasingly important for all facets of the business to keep focused on customer needs. The traditional model of a salesperson who focuses on customer needs and then negotiates with engineering to fulfill these needs as closely as possible is becoming less and less viable. The engineer must learn to be the salesperson. In fact, the entire company must become customer-centric.

A company can develop content and function that actually pushes the customer into the operation and workflow of the company. W. W. Grainger's Web site is a great example of this. The company realized that its catalog of goods for maintaining and repairing buildings, factories, institutions, and farms was difficult to use. So in creating the Web site, designers developed the award-winning Motor Match™ system to help customers choose from the company's selection of over 1,600 motors. The site invites the customer to click on a series of choices related to the types of motors that W. W. Grainger sells. Unlike a simple decision tree, in which a series of options is presented and depending on the one chosen, another series is presented, the motor match is free-form. In a free-form system, the decisions are not "irrevocable." You can pick motor voltage first, and then horsepower, or you can pick horsepower, then housing type, then voltage. After selecting the motor, the customer need only click the Buy button and the item is pulled and packed immediately from the nearest warehouse.

Infostructure Is More Important Than Infrastructure

The corporate infrastructure is a relic. The business world has spent decades debating the proper organizational chart. There is top-down, bottom-up, lateral, matrix. I've even seen a pizza-shaped organizational chart. But all this effort is meaningless if there is no organization of information, or *infostructure*.

Each time a customer uses interactive tools to communicate with a company, that interaction is an opportunity for the company to open a dialogue and instantaneously provide the customer with value. However, the ability of most companies to respond in a meaningful way to their customers is often constrained by one factor: the lack of management of knowledge collection, storage, and dissemination within their prospective businesses. Of course, this problem is exacerbated by the extremely fast pace of business on the Web.

Figure 1.1 demonstrates graphically where e-mail enters the company—at the intersection of

Figure 1.1 E-Mail Entry Point.

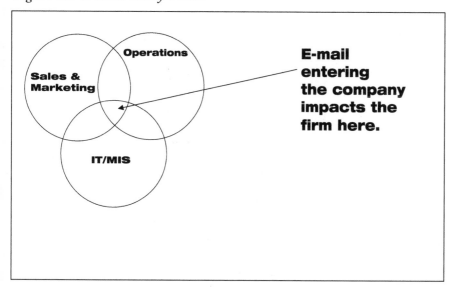

sales/marketing, operations, and information technologies. Stakeholders in each of these primary business areas can be affected dramatically. So who owns this customer information? Even more important, because this is happening in real time: How can the interests of all stakeholders be met simultaneously?

For example, imagine that a manufacturer of widgets gets an e-mail request for product specifications. Who answers? Engineering? Sales? The "Web master?" Clearly, they all have a role to play in communicating with this customer. But the customer doesn't want to hear from each department. The customer wants a single, authoritative answer to the question. Therefore, it is necessary to develop an information routing structure to answer the question, and quickly. This information may be from a person, a department, or even a database system.

An infostructuring initiative is essential. Developing an effective plan requires anticipating common questions and addressing the ownership of and approach to communications before getting to the technical details of routing a specific message. Chapter 6 addresses the development of an infostructure in more detail, but for now, you should be aware of three basic goals of an infostructure initiative:

1. To evaluate the way information and knowledge is originated, categorized, and routed within the company

2. To identify and eliminate redundant communications channels

3. To establish a clear "information authority"

Figure 1.2 demonstrates a typical approach to an infostructure. There is one information authority who "owns" the customer communication, but there are several sources of information—engineering, sales, and so on. Then in the final stage, there is one single action or implementation.

Figure 1.2 The Infostructure.

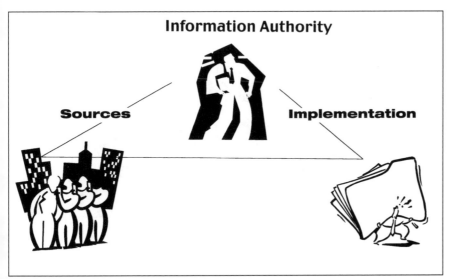

Information Authority

Sources

Implementation

Your Biggest Competitor Is Not Who You Think It Is

Electronic commerce speeds up the rate at which the competitive landscape can change. Interactive communication also introduces a new kind of competitor—the lateral competitor. Lateral competition occurs when companies outside the industry or sector set customer expectations.

Figure 1.3 illustrates the concept of lateral impact. This illustration has three key components: the sector, the functional aspects of that sector, and the lateral impact points.

The *sector* is the traditional competitive space in which the company does business. For example, Unilever would be in the packaged goods sector.

Figure 1.3 Lateral Competition.

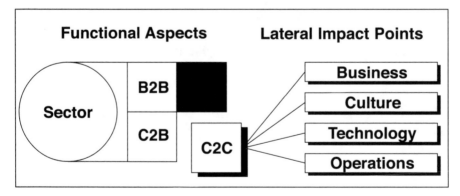

The *functional aspects* are the communications channels that can be employed within the sector. There are four core interactive communications channels a company must address (the two initiated by the consumer have become much more prevalent only through the emergence of interactive communications technologies).

1. *Business to Business (B2B)*—The working relationship the company has with suppliers, vendors, business partners, and others. This is a "trusted" relationship and usually involves "real" business transactions. Typically, these channels are closed and protected. In the interactive space, these channels are typically enabled through extranet projects.

2. *Business to Consumer (B2C)*—The "public" interface the company or company brands have with the consumer. It includes marketing, advertising, service before and after the sale, and the sales channel. In the interactive space, these channels are typically public Web sites and e-mail.

3. *Consumer to Business (C2B)*—A relationship made practical by large-scale interactive technologies, in which consumers "place" themselves as potential customers through proactive means or as a result of

a compensated relationship facilitated by a third party. Examples of this channel would be the request from a consumer to a business facilitated by Priceline.com or Mercata.com.

4. *Consumer to Consumer (C2C)*—Another communications channel made practical by large-scale interactive technologies. This is the channel in which consumers directly influence other consumers' decisions via one-to-one communications such as e-mail and instant messaging, or where a third-party facilitating organization leverages interactive communications technologies to enable a large number of people with similar likes or needs to communicate. Examples would include eBay and epinions.com.

For each of these four communications channels, there are four "lateral impact" points. These are aspects of the interactive relationship in which expectations set by outside (presumably non-competing) organizations can impact the customer-business relationship. These four pressure points are business, culture, technology, and operations.

1. *Business*—The basic business model upon which the organization is built. For

example, Dell is a "build when ordered" manufacturing business with a direct sales organization. Apple is a "build to forecasts" business with both a sales channel and a direct sales organization.

The various business models have their own advantages and disadvantages. However, the interactive communications channel may facilitate one model while hindering another. The business models that are facilitated by interactive communications cause lateral impact on a business model that is hindered by interactive communications.

Encyclopaedia Britannica is a perfect example of a company that lost business because it stuck to a business model that was hindered by interactive communications. Ironically, it was given the opportunity to partner with Microsoft to create a new product on CD-ROM. But Britannica's business model, sales force, and distribution were all geared to the sales of a multivolume book. The company refused Microsoft's advance. Microsoft then approached Funk and Wagnall's with the same business proposition. Britannica lost most of its market share and never recovered.

But the story does not end there. After a

time, Britannica decided to put the
encyclopedia online, but the company
was still unable to recognize trends in
electronic commerce. When it introduced its
online product, it decided to maintain the
traditional pricing structure of several
hundred dollars a year for access to the
material. Unfortunately, Britannica made
this decision just as the Internet was
becoming a mass-market phenomenon
with scores of companies providing
massive quantities of valuable
information "for free," supported by
advertising. Finally, in 1999, the
company decided to give in and "give
away" the information and support its
Web site with advertising. The results
were disastrous. The server was
hopelessly overloaded and countless
thousands of people were refused access.
But this story also represents yet another
business blunder. Just as Britannica was
switching to an ad-supported model,
paying for good information was
becoming more and more common. For
example, in March 2000, *Consumer
Reports* reported that they had over
370,000 paying subscribers on their Web
site. In the same month, *The Wall Street
Journal* had over 300,000 paid online
subscribers.

2. *Culture*—The culture consists of all
   the participants in an interactive
   relationship, both the target audience
   and the company itself. The group that
   feels comfortable with and empowered
   by the intrinsic capabilities of interactive
   communications will laterally impact the
   group that feels threatened or disem-
   powered by it.

   The Merrill Lynch story is an example of
   a company whose culture of full-service
   financial planning was in conflict with
   the culture of the customer base who had
   seen what it meant to do their own
   trades and were increasingly opening
   "experimental" accounts at the online
   brokerages.

3. *Technology*—The core technical
   capabilities of the organization are either
   enhanced by interactive communications
   or, in the case of lateral impact, are
   revealed to become a debilitating drag on
   the organization's ability to engage the
   target audience effectively.

   Lotus Notes was poised to take over the
   world in 1995. It was one of the first
   and most powerful information-sharing
   systems from Lotus, Inc. (now a unit of
   IBM). Unfortunately, to operate
   effectively, Lotus Notes required

advanced computers to act as servers and
extensive networks to connect them all
together, something that kept it from
becoming as popular as it might
otherwise have been. AT&T, seeing a
market opportunity, spent several million
dollars to develop a "public" Lotus Notes
server infrastructure across the United
States. Meanwhile, the far-less-powerful
Internet was growing rapidly. AT&T
pretty much ignored this "inferior" technology, which seemed to them to be
much less suited to the tasks of business
communications. But the Internet soon
pushed aside the public Lotus Notes
architecture in favor of Web servers and
Web browsers. AT&T scrapped the program, which had cost them several millions of dollars. While AT&T took a loss,
Lotus Notes was eventually reworked to
use the capability of the World Wide Web.

4. *Operations*—There are many methods
and practices of the daily operations of
the organization, from front-end
customer contact to back-office
accounting. For years, operating in
"batches" was perfectly acceptable. In
fact, letting small bits of work pile up
and then completing the workload all at
once would have been sensible for
companies that had small order volumes.
This model was widely duplicated in

other nonmanufacturing industries, such as insurance. In the insurance industry, it used to be common practice to set up an appointment with an agent, who would come to your home or office, ask some questions, and then mail a quote. This practice would be unthinkable today. Web sites such as Insweb.com not only provide quotes on demand but also offer comparison of policies and other services in real-time.

So it is important to carefully analyze threats to your market in terms of potential direct competitors. The electronic economy forces you to realize that lateral competition, although it may not always compete directly with your product, competes with your way of doing business. This is key to understanding how the electronic economy can make your company obsolete if you let it.

The Future Is Not What It Used to Be

Planning for the future has always been somewhat speculative, but you used to be able to rely on some fairly predictable models to forecast. Now, the relentless technological innovations that make up the intrinsic capabilities of the Internet seem to come so fast, it is hard to keep up with them all. Although there are incredible success stories of Internet start-ups, such as Yahoo! and Amazon.com, there are also massive failures, such as the original Microsoft Network and MagicCap, and less obvious failures such as the disappearance of hundreds of bulletin board services operated by local companies and the humbling of most online services (with AOL being the only exception). Many companies have seen their basic forecasting models looking remarkably obsolete.

Much of this disruption has been attributed to companies that don't "get it" when it comes to planning for the interactive future, but there have been few, if any, explanations of what "it" is. Let's take an approach that looks at the technological roots of learning what "it" is.

Traditional Assumptions. Traditionally, companies have used two basic curves to predict product sales, the technology adoption curve (Figure 1.4) and the product life cycle curve (Figure 1.5). Both figures show how a product may begin slowly, peak, and then decline in sales as the technology or product becomes obsolete. The technology adoption curve shows a chasm in the early adopter phase. This chasm is the market shift necessary to change a product's market from the few technically literate consumers to a market of mainstream buyers.[5] When a company predicts sales based on the combination of these two curves, it is making two primary assumptions, which do not seem to hold true in the fast-paced electronic economy.

Figure 1.4 Typical Technology Adoption Process.

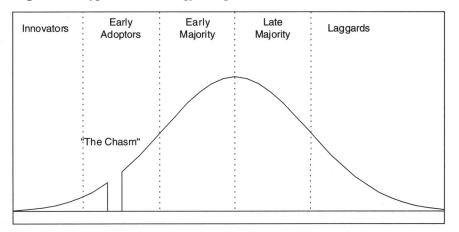

Figure 1.5 Typical Product Life Cycle.

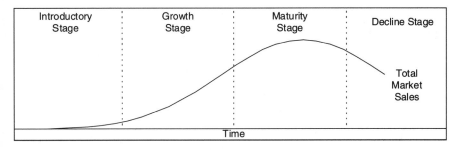

The first assumption is that the innovator of the basic technology can continue to gain benefit from the technology throughout the product life cycle.

Under the traditional product life cycle model, companies develop a product strategy that seeks to develop a "lock" on the consumer, making it difficult to switch to a competing product. One of the most common techniques is to engineer the product to work only within a certain "family" of products at all phases of the product life cycle. Consumers will incur heavy switching costs if they decide to change to a competing brand. Of course, this doesn't always happen. In fact, the plan can backfire.

The classic story of a battle to lock market share is the market-share war between VHS and Betamax. When videocassette recording capabilities first emerged, there was no standard. JVC, the innovator of the VHS format, recognized the importance of a standard, and the company was willing to dilute short-term profits to create a larger overall market for its format. They took a liberal approach to licensing their technology to many manufacturers. With a low cost of entry, many competitors emerged, but those competitors helped establish JVC's format, VHS, as the recognized industry standard.

Sony was more concerned with protecting the revenue stream from their technologically superior product. Betamax was only reluctantly licensed to competitors, and Sony made licensing of their format much more expensive. But this limited licensing meant that fewer Betamax VCRs would be on the market, so, naturally, fewer movies were put out in that format, which only reinforced the downward spiral of the product. Eventually, there was no market to be had for Betamax products. The lesson learned: A lock on a nonexistent market is worth far less than a share of a huge one.

The second assumption is that any competing products will have to start at the beginning of the product life cycle curve, thus allowing innovators to profit from the entire cycle of their original product.

It used to be a common assumption that a new technology would be just that, completely new. That newness meant there would be a significant "ramp-up" time before a product could be profitable, which shielded existing technologies from quick death. For example, the replacement product for vinyl records was the compact disk, or CD. The CD technology was completely new, requiring tens of billions of dollars in investment in infrastructure, from the CD pressing plants to the retooling of store display shelves.

Of course, Internet technology is bringing the physical barriers down and allowing new technologies to ramp up more quickly. The next innovative technology in the music industry is MP3 format music. It uses no physical media at all; music is on file on a computer. MP3 actually existed long before the Internet was widely

used, but the confluence of high-speed modems
and the Internet made it easy to distribute these
files. MP3 jumped to the middle of the product
life cycle with no replacement expenses.

**Product Displacement in the Electronic
Economy.** We've looked at typical forecasting
curves for new products or technologies. What
those curves do not reflect is the propensity for a
product or technology to be displaced. In the
electronic economy, it is very easy for a product,
technology, or established company to be displaced by a newcomer. How? Innovation cycles
are shortening, switching costs are being
reduced, expectations are rising, and barriers to
entry are coming down.

Figure 1.6 illustrates this concept in a general
form. In this scenario, Company X develops
product or service A, and Company Y develops
product or service B. The two products are quite
literally *identical*, and the delivery technology
for these products and services is ubiquitous.
What makes the difference is the way the business uses the tools themselves.

In this scenario, during the growth stage of A, an
innovation in product B displaces A by capturing
"mind share" of the early adopters. Company X
is unable to reap the rewards of its innovation
because of early displacement.

Figure 1.6 Early Product Displacement by Competitor.

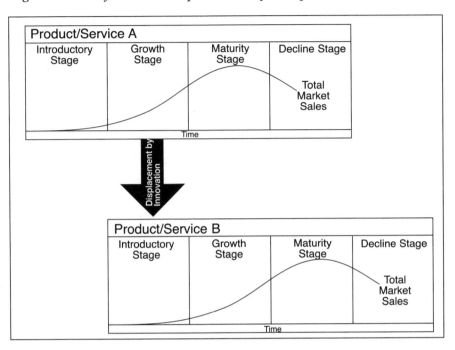

This scenario has been played out in real life. One of the best examples can be found in the very early Web browser market. Mosaic was the leading browser in the early stages of the World Wide Web. Netscape came along with a product that had some technical innovations, and not only did people respond to the innovation, they employed the Mosaic product to replace itself, using it to download free copies of Netscape!

The Internet also facilitates the trumping of established companies by upstarts. A classic

example is found in the little-known poetry pub-
lishers Blue Mountain Arts. Their site consistently rates in the top ten of all Web sites, offering customers electronic greeting cards. Yet
Hallmark.com, a leading "real-world" company,
does not even place on most lists of popular
sites? Why? Blue Mountain Arts claimed the
"innovation" phase of the product life cycle.
They were able to capture mind share of a con-
siderable user base and displace a major competitor. When Hallmark established a Web presence, they were unable to recapture the market
share because they did not have anything new to
offer.

Recall, also, the case of Microsoft and
Encyclopaedia Britannica. In that case, both
companies were established, but Microsoft was
able to gain market share through the innovative
application of technology.

Each of these three examples illustrates the value
of being perceived as an innovation leader, even
if a company is already a market, technical, or
financial leader. In each case, the tools or building blocks were commonly available. The difference was in the application of the tools.

This is the good news about the Internet. The
simple communications protocols that are building blocks of the Internet are available for any-

one to use. Nobody controls them. As a handful of phonemes can make up a rich language such as Chinese, the simple building blocks of the Internet can be used to build businesses that are profound or profane. The business concept itself may be proprietary, but the building blocks themselves are free. Perhaps most important, new (and far-more-powerful) building blocks continue to be developed and distributed for free by a community of technologists who are empowered and enabled by the existence of the network itself.

This activity means that the innovation phase of a business or product life cycle may be developed by an individual, a company, or a group of innovators. The business innovation is made available to all on the Internet—often at little or no cost—and with no switching costs.

Drivers of Innovation Successes. Of course, there is a positive way to deal with displacement: Displace yourself. Thus, the original company continues to benefit from innovation rather than be threatened by it. Figure 1.7 shows how a company might successfully retain market share through innovation.

There are four primary drivers of success in the innovation phase. The first, and possibly most important, is the concept of strong mind share.

Figure 1.7 Retaining Market Share through Innovation.

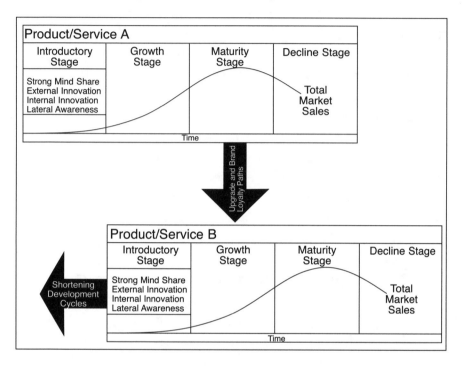

Basically, this is how smart or fast a company is perceived to be in the market. Sun Computer is quite good at developing mind share. Java was an orphan product left over from a failed interactive television project. But by being a champion and promoting the *concept* of Java—not the product—Sun has produced a tremendous pool of people inside Sun and in the business community at large who are ready, willing, and able to be innovators in Java.

The second driver of innovation success, external innovation, is the basis of Microsoft's success. Microsoft was not the original developer of MS-DOS, just the company that capitalized on it. Microsoft purchased MS-DOS and licensed it to IBM, gaining instant mind share for the product. Similarly, the whole concept of the graphical user interface was explored and developed by Xerox, but it was exploited and developed by Apple with the introduction of the Macintosh in 1984.

The third driver, internal innovation, is the result of recognizing and supporting new ideas and exploring all of the possibilities. The Nokia Corporation is a Finnish manufacturer, over 100 years old, known for superb wireless communications products. But Nokia started out as a company that made tissue paper! Later, Nokia made rubber boots, rubber bands, raincoats, and other rubber-related products. As the business evolved, it started making electrical cable, and this led to the development of radio equipment. By 1963, the company was innovating in radio telephones. While the manufacturer was involved in other industries, it relentlessly pursued internal innovation and rewarded those who developed ideas that became the foundation of the company. Today, Nokia is well recognized as a significant player in the worldwide wireless communications market. In twenty years, who

knows what Nokia will be making? But with a
culture of internal innovation, surely it will be
something unique and valuable.

Finally, lateral awareness is something that is
becoming increasingly important to all businesses. As with the earlier example of Encyclopaedia
Britannica and Microsoft Encarta, new and complex models of competition from traditionally
distinct markets are emerging. To avoid being
blindsided by unforeseen competition, companies must increasingly rely on complex and
seemingly improbable business models. Kmart,
AT&T, and Yahoo! now provide free Internet
service to the low-end market. In some suburban
markets, the local supermarkets compete not
only with one another but also with the local gas
stations. One-stop shopping is becoming more
popular in an accelerated society.

Concurrent Development. All of these effects
combined point to the need for a successful
modern organization to develop a product or
service that is in a continuous state of innovation. Companies must *never* let the product life
cycle enter the "decline" stage. Instead, they
must begin following a process of continuous
innovation and improvement. In this context,
that means that the service offered via the
Internet must be in a state of constant upgrade
while the business itself is in a state of constant

change. Together, these two concepts produce a "constant improvement curve," in which each product or service is upgraded and enhanced *before* it crests. This is *concurrent development.*

Figure 1.8 demonstrates the frequency with which a product or service must be replaced. It is no longer healthy to assume that one company can lock in a consumer through a product life cycle. A healthy company will realize that its product will be displaced and take upon itself the responsibility of presenting the next innovation.

A Note on Laggards. The emphasis here is on innovation. What, you might ask, about the market segment known as "laggards?" How can my product be completely displaced when there is such a large market of individuals who buy in

Figure 1.8 Concurrent Development Life Cycles.

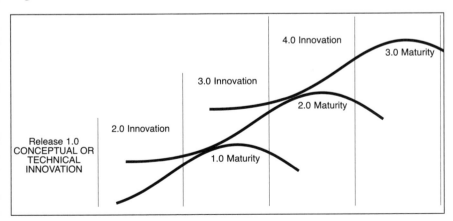

the last half of the product life cycle? The answer to that question is that even laggards have more technology and higher expectations than they've ever had.

The Internet newbie of today expects to own a device that connects to the Internet within five minutes of turning it on. She may have at least a basic idea of what a modem does (not necessarily how it does it) and will need to learn how to use some software products to some degree. Compare that to the early adopters of Internet connectivity, who had to know things like Serial Link Internet Protocol Scripting, Transmission Control Protocol, Internet Protocol Setups, and Modem Initialization Strings. The early adopters didn't have it easy, but their expectations were also low. They were interested as much in the *process* of connecting as in what to do when connected.

Today's newbies couldn't care less about the Internet, the modem, the network, and all of that. They want to go to a company online, see what they want, whether it be goods or a service, and they expect to be able to get it in a short, efficient transaction. They want to know what time the movie starts and how much the tickets are, and they will expect to buy them. They don't want to know about SSL, TCP/IP, FTP, HTTP, or anything else like that.

Companies that wish to capture the laggard market will not be able to push out old technology. It has to be better.

Summary

In each of the core concepts discussed, there are both opportunities and threats. It is important to understand that we are in the earliest phases of a fundamental shift in the nature of communications and commerce. The world of interactive businesses seems difficult for established companies to master, and there will be great failures of major organizations as a result. New, powerful companies will arise to take the place of the old ones. Yours can be the next Encyclopaedia Britannica, or it can follow the lead of companies that have learned to reinvent themselves, time and time again.

Over the next few chapters, we'll set out on a journey, one of discovery, introspection, and action. It's going to be a wild ride.

2

THE
WILD
KINGDOM

Introduction

Since there has been a fundamental shift in the business world, you must start by evaluating your own business fundamentals. What is the essence of your business? Is it suited to compete online? Where do you want your business to go?

In the middle of 1998, I was asked for the thousandth time that year to do a comparative study of Amazon.com, Dell, and a specific client. I had done this study so many times before that it had become rote, and rather than submit to another exercise, I challenged the client by saying that Amazon.com and Dell were structured in such a fundamentally different way from the client's organization that it was like comparing a fish with an antelope. Yes, they are both animals, but they just don't have much in common—and they compete in fundamentally different ways.

That analogy led to an extensive discussion of land-based animals (traditional businesses) versus aquatic creatures (Internet businesses). That, in turn, very quickly evolved into a simple, but effective, way of examining the nature of the core business models of various companies to determine how they can compete and thrive (or fail) in the interactive business environment.

The result of this thought exercise I call the *wild kingdom.* It's a tool that will be very helpful to you in quickly cutting to the core issues you need to address in developing your interactive business strategy.

Although there have been ample reports of the change to the business landscape brought about by the Internet, none have really analyzed the inhabitants of this landscape (the animals) and how they interact. The following conceptual discussion will help to provide insight into this new landscape and bring up some of the struggles and issues that face a company seeking to gain competitive advantage through the use of interactive communications.

The Landscape

Imagine the land as the world of traditional and established businesses and business models and the boundaryless water as the world of the Internet. Using this conceptual framework, we can develop a working metaphor for multiple business models. In our business landscape, we have five "animals," or business types: sharks, seals, whales, antelopes, and alligators. Each represents the essence of a different business model, although a company can have tendencies toward multiple animal types.

Sharks

The first animal in our conceptual menagerie is the shark. Sharks are those companies that are born of interactive technologies. These companies would quickly perish offline, in the traditional world of bricks and mortar. Put simply, a shark is a company that is made up of the following:

- A business model that can *only* exist online
- No equivalent or real competition offline

Profitable companies such as America Online, eBay, and Yahoo! were born of interactive technologies and capitalize on these technologies to lower operating expenses and improve profitability.

Unlike many companies that have simply adapted to the Web through electronic marketing and communications (e-marcom), e-service, and perhaps some e-commerce activities, shark companies have every aspect of their business defined, developed, and operated on the supposition that the customer is in control, that there are no switching costs to go from one company to another, and that speed in all aspects of the customer relationship is essential. Despite rumors to the contrary, sharks are already profitable or are very close to being profitable in the near future. As top predators in their environment, sharks are also known for quick acquisitions and being exceedingly fast.

Seals

Companies categorized as seals are also born of the Web. However, unlike sharks, seals are often outclassed both on land (offline) and in a confrontation with a shark in the water. Although they are well adapted to the Internet, once they have to compete with land animals, seals are neither fast nor formidable.

The easiest way to spot a company that is a seal is to see if it is trying to replace or mimic a well-established way of doing business with its online version. A seal simply comes up with a digital version of something that you can already do elsewhere with equal or greater ease. Either that, or the seal starts online but then begins to compete with strong land animals, and the seal will lose those battles. Think of a seal confronting a polar bear.

Prime examples of seal strategy were Pathfinder and Peapod. Pathfinder was a project of Time Warner (now AOL) to build a "superbrand" of online content from their stable of publications. Included in Pathfinder was content from *Time* magazine, *People* magazine, and *Sports Illustrated,* to name a few. After several years and tens of millions of dollars, Pathfinder was shut down. The imitation of magazines was not good enough to make consumers use the Internet for their news and entertainment. Peapod is a grocery delivery service that has been in business for years but has never managed to be profitable.

These companies are infamous for generating a buzz around the latest in online convenience they are promoting, yet they have been less successful at building strategies for long-term growth and profitability. Other seals include online "malls," which are neither better than bricks-and-mortar malls nor effective competitors with shopping sites like Buy.com and agent systems like MySimon.com.

Shoppers might be compelled to try a particular service simply for its novelty, but they are finding traditional offline modes more convenient and enjoyable. Seals, easily defeated by their land counterparts, will inevitably be outmatched online as sharks move into their space.

All seals are not doomed. In fact, seals may develop interesting and valuable businesses for a time, and a fat, happy seal makes an excellent meal for a shark. Planet All, an online date book and address book system, was devoured by Amazon.com, which sought to be able to get people gift-giving schedules tied to a reminder service. GeoCities, an online "community" of people publishing Web pages (basically a huge collection of self-published newsletters and magazines), was eaten by Yahoo! Yahoo! also acquired Broadcast.com (basically a TV and radio network) in a deal worth over $5 billion.

Whales

Whales spent a long time on the land before becoming sea creatures. Businesses in the whale category originally established themselves in the traditional offline world. However, they abandoned their offline positions to evolve and live in the water as pure Internet companies. Most whales safely coexist among the sharks.

These are companies with traditional, established business models that have been radically changed in order to leverage the capabilities of the Internet. In some cases this change was made for the sake of survival; in others, it was made simply because it was the most logical way for the company to continue as an ongoing concern.

Currently, the best example of a whale company is Egghead, which literally closed all bricks-and-mortar stores to sell online. There will undoubtedly be companies within the insurance, energy, banking, brokerage, and travel sectors that will also follow this course. A good example of a company that might be a whale in the future would be Keyspan Energy, one of the many independent electricity providers that does not own generating and distribution equipment. These companies are bringing customer need together with marketing services. Utility.com is already moving into this space.

Antelopes

On land, antelopes are fast and agile creatures able to move quickly from place to place, seeking fertile feeding grounds. They exist in vast numbers and tend to cluster in herds (or sectors).

Antelopes seem to be able to adapt quickly and move to meet changing business requirements. However, since they are so completely suited to the land, they do poorly in the Internet "water."

Certain companies must remain primarily land creatures, using the water for necessary sustenance, but not competing there. Taco Bell may sell promotional goods, hold contests, and conduct other interesting online programs, but their primary revenue will always be from in-person, in-store food sales.

Alligators

These ancient and powerful creatures are at home on the land or in the water. Alligator companies are typically old, strong, and highly adaptable to changing environments. They move deliberately, with a specific purpose, and are stunningly strong in battle. They are not choosy eaters, dining on fish or the occasional antelope that stops by for a drink. The most important fact about alligators is that they continually make the changing world around them work to their advantage.

Almost any business sector can include alligators. Companies categorized as alligators include

General Electric, Federal Express, L.L.Bean, J. Crew, and Wal-Mart. Sectors that have best facilitated entry into this category are finance, travel and accommodation, energy, and transportation. These companies see the Internet as an extension of their territory—new, fertile hunting grounds. They recognize the need to use different techniques on land and water. Companies and sectors in the alligator category are formidable competitors in all areas of business.

Where Do You Fit In?

In this "wild kingdom" of business, how can you tell where you company fits? Where do you want to fit? Although many people would say the shark or the alligator is the best business model to emulate, each of the other business models might also be an attractive and profitable option.

I have developed a simple tool to help you quickly assess your tendency toward one animal form or another. The evaluation factors for each "animal" are as follows:

- Selling methods
- Audience match
- Brand equity
- Distribution process
- Operational process

Figure 2.1 Company Business Model Benchmarking Worksheet.

Shark Score	Weight	Your Firm	Competition
1. What portion of total revenue is derived from Internet-based activities? (over 80% = 30))	30	0	10
2. Was the company started on the internet?	10	0	0
3. To what extent does the company offer a product or service that can't be duplicated off-line?	60	20	20
Possible/Total	100	20	30
Seal Score	**Weight**	**Your Firm**	**Competition**
1. To what extent is the business model based on existing customer behaviors?	35	20	5
2. To what extent is the business model based on replacing or displacing an existing non-information based business?	40	30	10
3. How "content" focused is the company?	5	5	0
4. How "community" focused is the company?	5	2	0
5. What portion of revenue is expected to come from online advertising?	15	5	5
Possible/Total	100	62	20
Whale Score	**Weight**	**Your Firm**	**Competition**
1. To what extent is the business based on information interaction?	20	20	0
2. Is the physical-world presence of this company typically a cost center?	10	0	0
3. To what extent can the company sell direct?	30	12	0
4. Does the company maintain a large (150+) call center?	10	10	0
5. To what extent can the company deliver effective customer service (including selling) over the phone?	30	10	5
Possible/Total	100	52	5
Antelope Score	**Weight**	**Your Firm**	**Competition**
1. To what extent is the company dependent on third party sales channels?	30	30	10
2. How extensive is the company's physical presence?	25	20	10
3. How much control does the company have over its distribution network? (No control = 10)	10	10	4
4. What portion of day to day operations are run by a fully integrated LAN/WAN? (less than 20% = 25)	25	7	8
5. Does the company have a commission-based sales force?	10	0	0
Possible/Total	100	67	32
Alligator Score	**Weight**	**Your Firm**	**Competition**
1. How frequently has the company completely transformed its business model? (1 or more in last 20 years = 10)	10	8	5
2. How long has the company been in business? (over 50 years = 10)	10	5	5
3. To what extent does the company rely on back-end systems to manage day to day operations?	35	22	10
4. To what extent does the company use ERP software?	10	8	6
5. To what extent does the company use sales force automation?	5	2	3
6. Has the company publicly stated its business objectives for the internet?	5	0	2
7. Has the company implemented and used EDI at any time?	10	0	10
8. To what extent does the company provide real-time customer service? (24/7/365 = 1%)	15	0	10
Possible/Total	100	45	51

- Interactive technologies (IT) capabilities
- Corporate culture
- Regulatory environment

The measurement process for the wild kingdom concept is quite simple. For each animal type, there are a number of weighted factors that drive the total score. Figure 2.1 is a complete business model benchmarking worksheet.[1] Sit down and score your own company as it relates to the competition.

For each evaluation criterion, a number of factors are assessed. Each factor is assigned a weight to reflect the relative importance of the factors. In every case, the business model has a maximum score of 100.

Scoring the Shark

The shark can be the easiest to spot. There are only three criteria, all based on the business's dependence on the Internet.

The first criteron is revenue. The less revenue derived from online activities, the lower the shark score. Internet-based revenue includes e-commerce or selling advertising on the Web. Eighty percent revenue was selected as a target because many shark companies derive additional revenue trading in their own stock.

Second, all sharks started on the Internet. This is a prerequisite to being a true shark.

Finally, there is the most subjective rating of them all: To what extent can products be duplicated offline? This can be a difficult assessment. Take eBay, for example. It can be argued that eBay, the online auction, is nothing more than a system of classified advertising, which is prevalent in other media. However, it is the unique quality of the Internet—the massive audience, the ease of interaction, the low costs of participation for the users of the system—that makes it impossible to duplicate in any other medium.

Another example would be Taco Bell. This company is obviously not a shark. It can't sell food online. But what if Taco Bell developed a "Taco Bell Kids Party" service for the online audience? You could connect to the Web site, create a menu, set a date and time, and pay for your party. Taco Bell would show up with a truck and a portable kitchen and you'd have a party. That would be very sharklike behavior. In this scenario, Taco Bell might rate a 30.

Scoring the Seal

The seal benchmark measures to what extent a business seeks to displace an existing acceptable customer behavior or acceptable business process.

The first two questions get to the heart of the matter (and thus make up 75 percent of the score). Seals don't use the Internet to change existing behaviors; they merely replicate them electronically. Seals move existing business models online. For example, they might use online order forms that look and function exactly like the offline version, without the ability to remember data so you never have to reenter your address again. Or they might list goods by item number like a product sheet. These are all indicative of seal models.

Scoring the Whale

The whale must be able to service the customer directly and at a distance. Information is most easily adapted to this model (question 1) Thus, insurance and finance generate high scores in this area. Of course, information is more than text on paper. Radio stations are in the information broadcasting business, and there are many radio stations delivering their information online. In fact, radio station waby.com is only on the Internet.

You can't be a whale unless you can service the customer directly. Customer service cost centers, direct-sales ability, large call centers, and phone-oriented customer service and sales are all aspects of that service. Companies that are particularly well adapted to these models might include electric utilities, banks, and government offices. Real estate and insurance are examples of industries in which it is difficult to sell directly. The intermediary is so entrenched that adaptation to the Internet is difficult. Furthermore, some industries find it difficult to sell without a personal touch. The auto industry is a perfect example. Although selling cars online is a rapidly growing business, there's still a need for customers to visit the showroom to test-drive the car, to see how the mirrors line up, get the feel of a car's performance, and so on. A more pure whale transaction might be renewing your car registration online.

Scoring the Antelope

Many companies don't want to be antelopes, but in reality, there are companies that simply aren't suited to being on the Internet except for support. The scoring of this section requires a clear understanding of the dependencies a company has on others for success: dependencies on third-party sales channels, physical presence, distribution networks, manual processes, and sales force.

Scoring the Alligator

Alligator scoring is based on some fairly standard business metrics. However, the criteria have been selected specifically because they reflect the flexibility necessary to "reinvent" a company while retaining the company's core value.

First, alligators are adept at making a complete transformation of the business. Many companies are not able to hold on to their value through a transformation of the economy. Examples include Grumman Corporation (now Northrop-Grumman), which was based on defense and aerospace contracting. Although Grumman did develop other product lines, such as aluminum canoes, commuter buses, and parcel delivery trucks, they could not survive the end of the cold war with their value intact. Another example is Pan Am. This airline was the de facto national carrier of the United States, but it failed to survive a deregulated airline ticketing market. Used to competing on service, not price, the company experienced a slow and painful decline, and with the bombing of Flight 103 over Lockerbie, Scotland, the company, already on shaky ground, folded.

On the other hand, there are many great companies that have survived extensive transitions of business models. General Electric has diversified, changed, and grown, and a leading part of the company's revenues comes from credit lending activities. Nokia, a leading maker of cellular telephone equipment, adapted for more than 114 years. They started out making tissue, were nationalized by the Finnish government, and then were denationalized. All along, Nokia rethought their plans and strategies and remained viable as an organization. They now make cellular telephone equipment.

Of course, to prove your ability to survive multiple changes, you have to be around a long time. Question 2 addresses the longevity of the company, and fifty years is chosen for benchmarking because most industries will have encountered significant change in that time frame.

Third, the employees of the company must trust the computer more than paper. Employees working with enterprise resource planning (ERP) systems, sales force automation, and electronic data interchange (EDI) might be more inclined to trust the computer, rather than paper, for the majority of their tasks. Industries such as airlines and hotels rely on extensive real-time "back-end" systems to manage reservations and other critical business activities. On the other hand, there are retail organizations that still rely heavily on paper trails and manual systems for day-to-day activities.

ERP systems manage the flow of information related to operations throughout the organization. Ample stories exist of failed and astonishingly expensive implementations of these systems that track and automate everything from raw goods procurement to end-user billing. In many cases, these attempts failed because the company implementing ERP failed to understand the complexity and training requirements of ERP systems. A successful implementation of ERP indicates a candidate for the alligator group.

A company must publicly state its business objective for the Internet. Some folks would see this as an odd benchmark, but the purpose is simple: to establish that there is a vision for the Internet in the future of the company and that the vision is clear enough to be shared with the public.

Finally, the hours of operation might seem unimportant, but I've found them to be critical in today's economy. Most businesses do not operate around the clock, and learning the complexities of doing so is difficult. However, an alligator will need to be always open for business in order to maintain flexibility in future transitions.

Concluding the Evaluation

When you are scoring yourself, be sure to score your competition as well. When you have determined your series of scores and your competitors' scores, you can plot them on a simple radar chart to better understand your relationship in the marketplace.

A radar chart shows comparative values of several concurrent criteria on a polar coordinate chart. It is most useful when comparing many criteria concurrently, and best to use when five or more criteria must be considered at the same time.

You can use Microsoft Excel to create a radar chart like the one shown in Figure 2.2. You can also download this spreadsheet at www.facazio.com/efactor.

Do you come out a little more seal-like? Is your competition is a little more of an alligator? This result tells you to be careful not to get gobbled up.

Figure 2.2 Business Model Benchmarking Results.

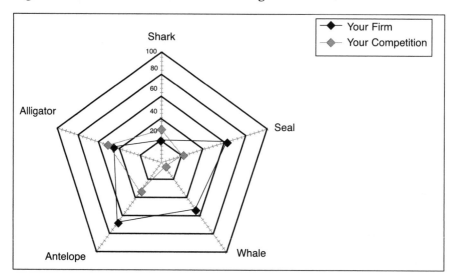

Summary

The landscape we have just drawn does more than tell you who you are in relation to your competition. It shows you what your options are. You need to decide which animal characteristics best fit your vision and your industry. Becoming a shark or an alligator might seem most enticing, but there is a place in this world for whales, seals, and antelopes as well. For example, the restaurant business has a physical component that cannot be changed. No one wants virtual food. So a restaurant will never be a shark. But restaurants are also an entire experience (reservations, service, atmosphere, entertainment, and so on), and portions of that can be brought into the electronic era. And, of course, you want to stay one step ahead of the competition.

If you are 100 percent satisfied with your position in the landscape, you can put down this book right now. But if you are like most companies and want to change some characteristics, if not animal types, keep reading. It's time to learn how to morph!

3

THE
BUSINESS
PLAN BEGINS

Introduction

The five-year plan—what a wonderful relic of days gone by! In the same way the Communist Party learned it is impossible to decree what the potato harvest will be in five years, business today is learning it is impossible to rely on specific long-range plans in the interactive business world. Trying to create a five-year plan for your online business is like trying to delineate a five-year plan for the weather.

In this chapter, I will introduce a planning strategy that will help your company approach a volatile business horizon. Like most other methods, this business planning method focuses on three steps:

1. Evaluating the business environment
2. Setting business objectives
3. Establishing metrics and measures of success

You might, however, find this method somewhat uncomfortable: It looks at only a one-year horizon. Why only one year? Because anything beyond that is just speculation. When we look at how quickly the competitive environment is changing, we realize that the purpose of a business plan should be to give direction and monitor success, but not to dictate specific practices. Therefore, this planning methodology focuses on maintaining the agility necessary to change.

Evaluating the Business Environment

Before you begin setting your business objectives, you need to understand where the market is going. I've developed a graphical framework that will aid in projecting the changing environment. You start by looking at *overall* online business capabilities and how they change over time. In Figure 3.1 the vertical axis represents the set of online business capabilities and the horizontal axis represents time.

The first thing to put on the graph is the current state (time = 0). Data for this feature is obtained through observation of the interactive world. Look at online business practices in general, not at a specific company. And look for a "blended best of breed" set of expectations. After all, your clients don't just compare you to your competitors; they skim along from Amazon.com to CNN to Dell to eToys, and so on. Customer expectations for product and service selection, customer support, and Web site performance are set by the market leaders. Figure 3.2 shows how these expectations rise over time and indicates, as we enter the early 2000s, that these expectations are not likely to be reduced in any way.

You then can look out six to twelve months to those "cutting-edge" capabilities and concepts that are beginning to crop up in real-world applications. They might not be marketable now, but these technologies could easily impact your company within the next year. Figure 3.3 shows what this part of the graph might look like early in the new millennium.

Figure 3.1 Online Business Capabilities over Time.

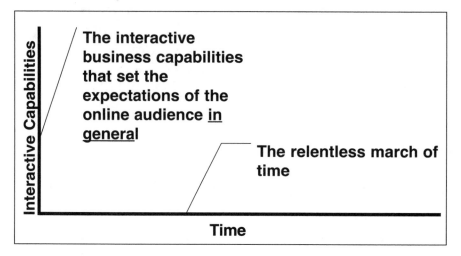

Figure 3.2 Current State Online Expectations.

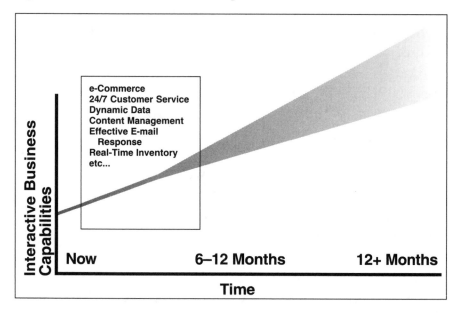

Though you can't be certain about the direction these technologies might take the market, you can recognize the need to monitor their progress and adjust your own interactive capabilities accordingly over the next six to twelve months. You can also hedge bets now on the kind of work you should be prepared for in the near future.

Finally, you can plot those technologies you expect to be marketable twelve months or more from now. Of course, this estimate is little more than informed speculation, but it does help you to keep an eye on those capabilities that are currently interesting but are fairly far over the horizon and not directly impacting the business. By looking at seemingly far-out ideas and capabilities and thinking of them in the context of the future business direction and needs, you can begin to stitch together a long-term view of the business possibilities through scenario planning. Figure 3.4 shows what this plot might look like in early 2001.

Now that you have established a set of common environmental expectations, you can plot your current state. Where are you in relation to the current set of expectations, and at your current rate of change, where will you be six to twelve months from now vis-à-vis these expectations? Are you on a path leading to parity with interactive expectations? If not, your graph might look

Figure 3.3 Cutting Edge Online Expectations.

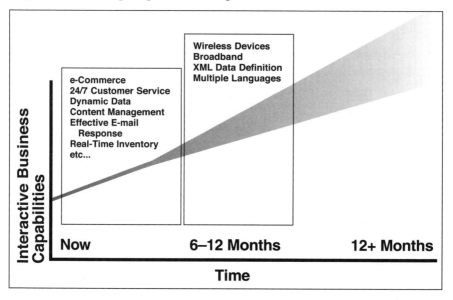

Figure 3.4 Speculative Expectations.

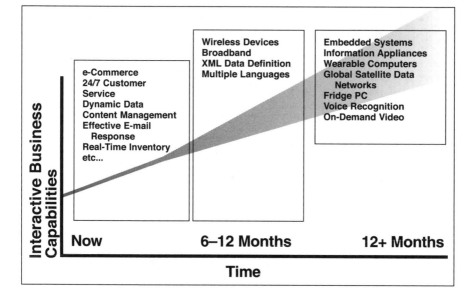

something like Figure 3.5, and you would want to make some adjustments.

While it's important to measure yourself against a common set of expectations, it is also important to identify the position of direct competition. Start with your traditional competitors. For example, Ford might look at GM or Daimler Chrysler. As they found out, they needed to partner with each other to catch up. Your current competition might be above or below the current set of expectations, just as you might be. If all competition is below the curve, this fact would leave the market wide open for a new entrant. On your graph, identify the current state and path of traditional competitors.

Figure 3.5 Corporate Online Capabilities.

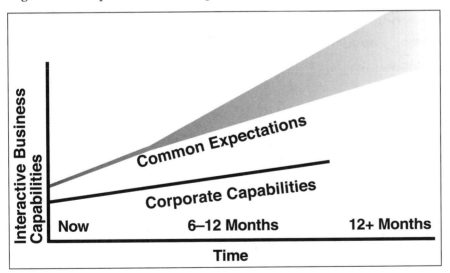

Next, try to predict where new competitors will
enter the market. New entrants often enter the
fray when the current competitors in an industry
are not fulfilling common expectations. I've
already discussed the case of Encyclopaedia
Britannica in Chapter 1. The company was actually technologically capable of fulfilling expectations, but it chose not to do so. Another example
would be car dealerships. Historically, there has
been very little competition for car dealerships
from the online world until the emergence of
Autobytel.com.

Car dealerships are a great example of an industry being forced to follow rules set by other companies. It is safe to say, I think, that most people
view buying a car with the same enthusiasm they
would have for tooth removal without anesthe-
sia. In the case of car dealers, before the Internet,
the concept of "price transparency" was pretty
much nonexistent.

A company called Auto-by-Tel had been selling
cars over the phone for some time, but the
Internet unleashed their real power: giving customers the ability to see what the dealer paid for
a car before buying. Auto-by-Tel simply prequalified customers by determining their needs and
showing them the available options. They then
sent the lead to a car dealership, charging the
dealer a fee for the lead. Even as recently as

1996, this was unheard of. Now, even Amazon.com is selling cars online.

In other words, now auto dealerships have a sizable competitor in the online market that is encroaching on their traditional sales. As you complete this picture, you will be able to analyze the competitive environment six to twelve months from now with much greater ease (see Figure 3.6).

Finally, remember to do a quick analysis of some scenarios that combine the seemingly random technologies and capabilities you see on the horizon. The music industry has seen a surprising (to many) convergence of MP3 technology and instant messaging that is changing the face of the industry. Good industry analysts might have looked at MP3, but nobody prepared for the convergence of these technologies.

MP3 is a standard for recording high-quality audio to computer files. It is a free, open standard; anyone can use it. Best of all, the compression algorithms used for MP3 produce relatively small files. Music on compact discs can be converted to an MP3 file easily, and the software to do it is free.[1] MP3 (and the up-and-coming MP4, which offers similar functionality for audio and video) was a "distant horizon" technology in 1998.

Figure 3.6 Potential Competitive Capabilities.

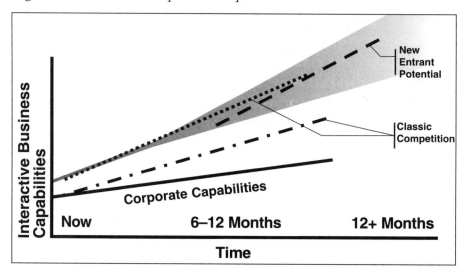

In 1999, faster 56K modems, faster computer processors, and very large and cheap hard disks were all separate technological advances, which, taken individually, had a range of fairly predictable uses. Among these uses were the creation of MP3 digital audio files and their storage on Internet-connected computers and distribution over the Internet. This model, while somewhat new to the music industry, is relatively controllable, because the files on a publicly accessible Web server can be examined by automated technologies that scan for files that are copyright violations. In fact, almost as fast as people (usually college students) put up a Web server full of MP3 files of every song ever recorded by the Rolling Stones, the server is quickly found and a cease-

and-desist letter is sent out, forcing the removal of the Web site.

The real disruptive horizon technology is instant messaging. Instant messaging is wildly popular on America Online (AOL). It allows short text messages to be sent from one person to another or from one person to an ad hoc group of people in real time. Until recently, however, AOL members could send instant text messages only to other AOL members. Meanwhile, other instant messaging technologies, most notably a product called ICQ, were released. ICQ worked with *any* Internet-connected computer. To gain competitive advantage, ICQ added the ability to *send files* as well. To maintain market share, AOL quickly bought ICQ, and added two vitally important features to its instant messaging system. First, it let anyone, even non-AOL members, have the free software needed to send instant messages over the Internet. Second, it added the "file transfer" capability to its instant messenger software.

Suddenly, instant messaging, a horizon technology at best, begins to affect the recording industry. How? Using the ad hoc group communication feature of the instant messaging software, huge communities of people, using their fast computers and modems, are now able to share their music files nearly instantly by sending them directly from person to person using their instant message system. This is called peer-to-peer (P2P) networking. MP3 files are no longer stored on a publicly accessible server; they are on an individual's computer. The music industry's automated technologies that track down illegal files on public servers do not work anymore.

The music industry is understandably up in arms over this new entrant into their industry. Imagine a virtual community in which many people "chat" about music. During these chat sessions, a nearly continuous stream of requests ("Anyone got the new Jewel song?") is presented to the group, followed by many responses ("sure, sending 2 u now"). The instant messenger clients send the files from consumer to consumer. Fast modems make it easy. The record companies have no ability to stop the transfer of these files.

Napster, the music-sharing company, is currently in a huge legal battle over its software, which facilitates the creation of P2P networks.

The music industry did not envision or plan for this reality. They are only now attempting to develop secure digital music files with encryption to prevent duplication. But virtually every CD ever made is source material for conversion to MP3 files, and the exchange of these files will continue to grow.

With a good horizon plan, the music industry could have actually recognized and leveraged these communities. Products like low-cost, high-quality music files or subscriptions to advance releases of the latest music could have been offered by the recording companies themselves.

Even though the music files would eventually leak onto the network anyway, the recording studios would have been able to obtain a good revenue stream by leveraging the early adopters.

Setting Business Objectives

With the chart in front of you, it's time to set business objectives. Of course, your goal should be to meet or exceed the common environmental expectations that you have laid out. How do you attempt to do so? The answer to this question, like so many questions in life, is *one step at a time.*

First, look at the current state gap. There are many things you can change immediately that will bring you on par with expectations. In Figure 3.7, these are the A-level changes. Typically, these are process management changes, not technology changes. A frequent example of an A-level change would be to improve e-mail response time to one hour.

Level-B changes are those with a two- to three-month time frame. For example, your customers are probably expecting some form of electronic commerce, and you can get this to them relatively quickly. Keep in mind that the expectations will be somewhat higher in two to three months, so your goal should be to meet those requirements.

Level C incorporates enterprisewide changes. These changes can take six to twelve months to complete. You might, for example, find that within the next six to twelve months you will need to tie together your call center operations and e-mail responses. You want to start planning for these eventualities now so that you will have

Figure 3.7 Launching Strategic Projects.

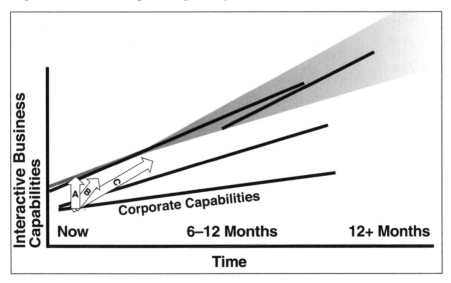

the operation up and running in the prescribed time frame.

In yet another case of e-commerce making strange bedfellows, the Big Three auto manufacturers—Ford, GM, and Chrysler—are, at this writing, developing an online procurement system. They each looked at the common set of environmental expectations in the procurement function and realized that they could not reach those expectations through individual efforts. Instead, they're in the process of forming a fourth company (owned equally by the three automakers) to effect an industry change. All suppliers to the auto industry, whether they make engines or seats, will be required to hook into an interactive procurement system. This system will include specifications, pricing, and other data, and all buying decisions will be made using this proprietary system.

Establishing Metrics and Measures of Success

There are two parts to this final step: establishing specific goals for interactive communications and establishing metrics to measure the success. Clients often come to Web developers saying they want to get on the Web to "build awareness" or "have an Internet presence," but these goals are not specific enough to provide direction. Start with the map you've just built of the business environment. Where do you need to go? Then ask yourself the five w's—who, what, where, why, and when—to drill it down one level. Whose awareness are you trying to build—employees, certain market segments, other? What do you want to build awareness of—specific product lines, company vision, something else? When do you need that awareness achieved? Remember, a Web site can improve sales, aid marketing activities, reduce costs, communicate important messages, and do many other things. That's why specificity is essential.

The Corcoran Group, a New York City real estate company, provides a good example of a business that uses a worthy approach to building an Internet presence. It went into the process with a specific objective: to generate prequalified sales leads. There are two important parts to this goal: (1) to generate leads and (2) to prequalify those leads before the real sales expenses are generated. Therefore, the Corcoran Web site provided potential customers with exceedingly detailed and interactive information about properties for sale, including photographs and 360-degree panoramas of the interiors of the properties. The company developed tools to help potential customers evaluate how the property would fit their needs. The Corcoran Group reports that in 1995, their first year to operate the Web service, $4.9 million in sales were initiated through qualified leads gathered on the Web site that year. By 1997, $60 million in sales were qualified through the Web service, and the numbers continue to grow.

Figure 3.8 gives a few examples of some not-so-good Web goals that one might think are good at first glance. Why aren't they good? Because, although they all represent positive direction for Web activities, they are not specific enough to provide good yardsticks of success. The corollary "good Web goals" listed all have something in common: They are quantified and have an established time frame.

Measuring Performance

The biggest myth about the Internet is that it is not measurable. In fact, the Internet is far more measurable than most other communications methods. For example, the demographic profile of newspaper readers is based on statistical interpretation of a small sample of people who are asked about their reading habits. These interpreted results are taken as facts when presented in a demographic report. For example, many reports claim women aged 34 to 50 read a specific section of the paper. In actuality, *some* women aged 34 to 50 told someone who called them on the phone that they read that section. Everything is presented through the filter of the question asked, the sample size, and the quality of the interpretation.

Figure 3.8 Goal Setting.

Not-so-good Goals	Good Goals
Reduce costs	Reduce paper document distribution costs by 30% by 3rd Quarter 2000
Improve sales	Get 25% of all revenue from Internet sales by 2002
Increase awareness	Increase awareness of our product among employees by 25% by the end of 2nd Quarter 2000
Increase number of hits	Get $5 Million in sales prequalified through the Web site by 4th Quarter 2000

Although this kind of measurement is useful, it just can't compare to the fact-based measurement possible with Internet-delivered information. In fact, with the Internet there's too much data provided, and a whole new strategy of measurement must be developed to use the flood of data effectively.

The Web Server and Log Files

The World Wide Web was originally intended as a way for people to collaborate on a project. It was developed in a science lab where it was necessary for various teams to have easy access to information without the bother of having a user name and password on every computer in the facility.

Thus, the basic premise of a Web server is to quickly and anonymously provide information to any computer that "asks." Web servers maintain records of each and every file that is sent from the server to the Web browser. This generates an astonishing amount of statistical data for even a moderately trafficked Web site.

Measurement and interpretation of Web site statistics is often an exercise in frustration. There is so much raw data and so many tools that purport to interpret the data that it is easy to lose the strategic emphasis in measurement.

In most interactive development projects, the Web development team works with a set of basic statistical objectives for the Web site that can be easily measured with server log file analysis. Figure 3.9 is a list of typical statistical Web goals.

One of the biggest mistakes I've seen is the tendency to use Web server statistics as the *only* basis for performance measurement. Much more can be done to measure Web site performance when the measurement strategy is developed in a way that accounts for business goals and is integrated with business processes.

Measuring the actions of a Web server fulfilling requests for various bits of text and images by Web browsers is not a measurement strategy; it is a way of producing information. What is needed is a way to take the information and turn it into knowledge. "Number of hits" is an interesting indicator, but it doesn't paint a complete picture.

Figure 3.9 Typical Statistical Web Goals.

1. Increase overall site traffic by 15%
2. Increase sales lead traffic by 50%
3. Ensure all visitors return at least once in every 30-day period
4. Decrease site downtime to 1% of all uptime
5. Know who is visiting the site by increasing the number of registered users
6. Measure P&L accurately
7. Increase positive site comments by 20%
8. Increase qualified leads by 10%
9. Increase sales through the Web site

The real question is, "How many of the 100 million people using the Internet every day can I convince to move from being a potential customer to becoming an actual customer?" or "How is the Web site affecting the ongoing relationship with the customer?" Remember, the Web site is an integral part of the business. It is subject to the same performance measurement criteria as any other part of the business.

Would you use the volume of telephone calls coming into an entire company as a performance measurement for that company? Although this number is of some interest, it is not as important as other measures you might include in a scorecard. There is simply too much noise built into the measure.

So then, would the number of calls coming into a dedicated customer service call center be of value? This is intrinsically linked to the mission and strategy of the call center. However, even the number of incoming calls is less relevant than the nature and outcome of the calls. Identifying, say, an increase in calls from customers with a specific problem is much more valuable than identifying an overall increase in calls.

The scenario on the Internet is identical. Server log file analysis tools measure the action of transferring the files that make up a Web "page" from one computer to another—the incoming calls. But technology now allows us to capture more detailed information about the online customer relationship. Sites have become more personalized and database-driven. It is not practical to think of a Web site as a series of pages that the user "views." This model is only applicable to the earlier models of Web page development, where there is static hierarchy of text and graphic files from which Web pages are constructed. A more refined site development strategy builds an interactive interface utilizing personalization, integration of live and dynamic data, and traditional content in the form of pages and downloadable media. In this kind of Web site, there is less concern with the specific actions taken by the server in fulfilling the user's request for the page assembly elements than there is with the actions taken by the users of the Web site.

A Strategy for Measurement and Assessment

The strategy, then, is to find the valuable business measures that relate to Web server activities.

To find them, start by listing your strategic goals in the left-hand column. From each of these goals, brainstorm a list of tactical measures that might help you determine whether you are meeting these goals. Figure 3.10 gives an example of what your chart might look like.

Remember, the valuable measures will not focus on the content of the site, but on the relationship with the customer, that is, the customer's response to and interaction with the site. Figure 3.11 is a diagram of a Web site. Methods for accessing the site can be found at the top of the diagram. Customer interactions are defined by the arrows. Finally, the point at which your audience reaches a specific content area is shown at the bottom of the diagram. The relationship that you wish to measure is in the transitions (or

Figure 3.10 Strategic Goals and Tactical Measures.

Strategic Goals	Tactical Measures
Improve customer service through the creation and effective operation of an interactive communications system that is available 24 hours a day, 7 days a week.	• Increase overall site traffic by 15% • Increase sales lead traffic by 50% • Decrease site downtime to 1%
Develop a personal relationship with the individual using the service and provide that user with individualized and relevant information that meets their needs.	• Know who is visiting the site • Ensure all visitors return at least once 50% of the time • Increase positive site comments by 20%
Demonstrate an effective return on investment for the project.	• Measure P&L accurately • Increase qualified leads by 10% • Increase sales from the web site

Figure 3.11 Web Site Flow Chart.

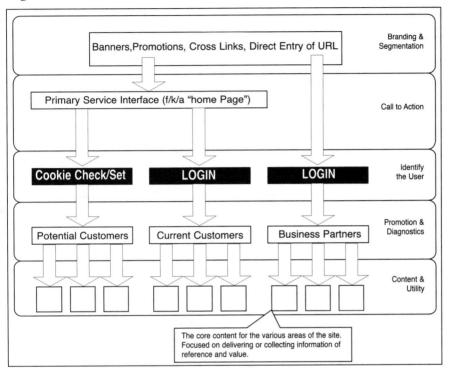

arrows)—when they access the home page, log in, or interact with specific content.

For example, a company may determine that repeat visitors are particularly valuable and begin measuring repeat visitations against a target objective. In this scenario, it is not so important to measure the specific pages that the repeat visitor is using, because the actions taken by the user will be ample evidence of the success or failure of the design, content, and functionality of the site.

Ultimately, the measure is of the effect of the site on the whole business, not just the individual components or the specific assets, such as a "page" or particular graphic. Should there be a reason to drill down to the more atomic level of data on specific files or graphics transferred from the server to the user, the data will always be available for review.

There are a number of tools that can be used to measure your Web site's contribution to the business. Chapter 9 discusses some of those tools in more detail. But keep in mind that the necessary data will be much easier to collect if the capability is built into the Web site from the outset. For that reason you must discuss measurement before a Web project is initiated. Developing a measurement strategy in concert with a production process will provide a more effective set of basic data from which interpretive results can be drawn.

Coordinating with the Enterprise

Although your Web site is inherently measurable, the structure of your company might be a hindrance to measurement. In many companies, Web activities are compartmentalized. If you don't coordinate the Web business with other parts of the business, you can't measure its success. I can't stress this enough: *If you want to measure the impact of the site on your business as a whole, your Web activities will need to be viewed as part of the business as a whole.* For example, if you don't coordinate with the sales department to track those sales that come in from the site, you will not know the full effect of your Web activities on sales. You may need to ask other important questions of the sales department as well. Perhaps your site doesn't generate many direct sales but it does an excellent job of pre-qualifying the leads. Can Web server statistics tell you this? No. It must come from the salespeople who deal directly with those Internet-generated leads.

Another example might be integrating services with your normal customer services operations. There is an all-too-true advertisement for IBM that pictures a woman who ordered an item online being unable to cancel it over the telephone. This case shows the results of compartmentalized e-commerce activities. Unfortunately, this company is not able to track whether there are customer problems arising specifically from electronic commerce because of the barrier that exists between e-service and other forms of customer service.

A manufacturer might also be capturing very important measurement data as packages are scanned on the loading dock, but a compartmentalized Web department might not be able to access that data.

Fortunately, many parts of your company are probably already accustomed to integrating media tools with the rest of your business. If you find you have to wage an integration campaign, these are typically good places to start. Generally speaking, the departments that will be the most receptive are those that are closest to the customer. Public relations or communications departments are often very technology-savvy. Human resources departments are becoming increasingly accustomed to integrating various tools for recruiting purposes. Many now post on sites such as monster.com or careermosaic.com and are accustomed to receiving résumés electronically as well. Other departments that integrate technology may not be what you would consider traditional corporate mouthpieces. For example, employees at the warehouse may have some of the best ideas about typical customer problems with products. As you are able to integrate your operations with the most receptive areas, you will want to gradually work more closely with knowledge originators, those who are creating the information.

Continually Planning

One final note: Remember that your planning horizon will never get closer. What do I mean by that? There will always be looming technology and possible new entrants during the six- to twelve-month window. So you can never stop planning. Let's say you were originally targeting your e-commerce efforts at customers who primarily use Palm Pilots. But then there's a change on the horizon that looks like using broadbanding is really the way to go. If you continue in your original plan, you will find yourself marketing to only a small segment of the market. And twelve months from now, any changes to the plan will be extremely expensive. If, instead, you alter your plans now, the change may actually be relatively minor. Figure 3.12 illustrates how a one-degree change to your current path results in a significant position change in twelve months. You can stay agile as a company by constantly keeping your eye on the horizon and making minor adjustments as needed along the way.

Summary

This planning method is specifically designed to help you think through the needs that electronic commerce presents. Specifically, you will need to become comfortable with short planning horizons that necessitate agility on the part of your company. Of course, these are not just technology plans. These are business plans you are making. Calling electronic sales e-business is akin to calling faxed orders f-business or telephone sales

Figure 3.12 Effect of Minor Change Today.

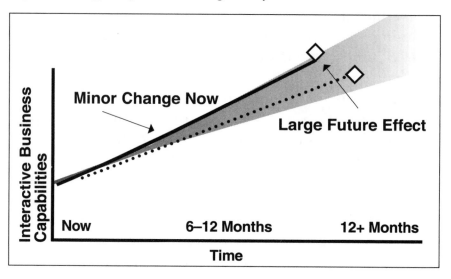

t-business. Electronic commerce is a part, albeit an extremely important one, of your overall business plan, and this planning methodology should incorporate your overall business goals.

Thus, the core business planning strategies are as follows:

1. Analyze the environmental expectations for the market as a whole, whether defined by your direct competitors, lateral competitors, or new entrants.
2. Define your business goals and required path based on your current and projected shortfalls.

3. Coordinate the development of the site in the context of overall business plans and needs.

4. Continually assess the effectiveness of these efforts in generating the specific results required.

5. Define general business goals and assessment metrics and relate these metrics to the performance of functional areas of the site by measuring the transitions and behaviors of the user.

As in the other parts of your business, you will never reach completion of your business plan. You are always planning for the next environmental shift.

4

THE ONLINE AUDIENCE

![Introduction section marker] Introduction

Everyone is online. Well, not really everyone. Over 50 percent of the world's population has never made a phone call, much less gone online. But in the United States, the Internet is being adopted far faster than any other technology. Although estimates vary significantly, it has been widely reported in the media that the telephone had 50 percent United States population penetration seventy years after initial commercial deployment; the television after thirty years; the automobile after twenty-five years; and the Internet after five years (the early days of the Internet were strictly noncommercial). Such a large percentage of people in developed nations are either online or will be shortly that the online target audience is not substantially different from the offline audience. The typical Internet user is no longer male, young, and affluent. Users are the same type of people you have always served. They are either customers or people who should be your customers.

The question, then, is not, "Should we address the needs of the online audience?" You are already marketing to members of the online audience, albeit through traditional means. The question becomes, "How do we meet the needs of a specific market segment online?"

How the Online Audience Changes Your Business

Even though your customers are the same ones you've always known, their habits have changed now that they have been exposed to the world of e-commerce. They are demanding, value speed, and have a disheartening lack of loyalty. The large brokerage companies discovered this lack of loyalty. Many people who had been with the same broker for twenty-five years switched to electronic trading because switching costs were so low. Customers may get accustomed to certain processes or services they can get online. A purchasing agent who's had a long-standing relationship with one supplier may choose to switch to freemarkets.com to buy goods from the open market. Your customers might have been happy with faxing in orders instead of mailing them. But now that they've had a taste of electronic commerce, they don't want to fill out forms at all. They much prefer a system that remembers their customer information so they don't have to enter it each time. Now faxing order forms is a negative for these customers.

On a personal note, I no longer use the large travel agency that I used to use because I get tired of repeatedly giving them all the information they request. Instead, I go to biztravel.com, whose system remembers me, my preferred airports, and other relevant information. I can get plane tickets with a complex itinerary while simultaneously taking care of my customers on the phone.

The Internet also allows you to reach new audiences you never intended to reach. You may be targeting current customers with your site, but other groups such as job seekers or investors will also be visiting it. These "read-only" audiences don't need heavy interaction, but you do need to be prepared for their visits.

Not only is nearly everybody in the United States online, but the global online audience is tremendous. The year 1998 was the last one in which English-speaking people represented a majority of Internet users. In 1999, according to Forrester Research, the largest and most respected e-business research firm in the world, only 50 percent of the users of the Internet were English speakers. By 2003, this number is expected to decline to about 34 percent. If you weren't before, you are now a global company.

Defining Your Audience

Because you can reach almost anyone with your Web site, you must start by defining the primary audience or audiences you wish to reach. Start at the broadest level. Are you trying to reach customers, potential customers, employees, vendors, business partners, investors, and so on? Your goal should be to find the valued subsets— the groups that will actively use the service, gain value from it, and provide value back to the organization.

Finding these valued subsets isn't as easy as it may sound. They may not be who you expect them to be. Looksmart (www.looksmart.com), a service of *Reader's Digest*, started out as a general-purpose directory of sites on the Internet. Over time, they discovered that the majority of people using their site were women. They had to redefine their understanding of whom they were serving.

Once you define the valued subsets, you need a focused definition of these users. Analyze how these groups are accessing your site. Are they using broadband access or modems? Agency.com has done an excellent job of segmenting their customers. Their most profitable customers are large corporations with broadband connections. They immediately hit you with QuickTime movies when you log onto their site. Why? First, because that's what their customers expect. But this strategy has an additional benefit. They are actually able to prequalify customers by weeding out those with modems, who are likely to be unprofitable customers.

You might want to place each of your target audiences on the audience quadrant (see Figure 4.1). Assess your target audiences on their level of awareness of your brand and your site and their likelihood of seeking for you. Of course, your goal will be to move everyone to the top right-hand quadrant. The "seeking-aware" are your most active customers.

Unaware Audiences

This audience needs to learn about your company, products, and services. You will need to provide educational and introductory content. Don't forget, however, that information alone is not enough. There has to be something "in it" for the audience, a value for them that makes it worth any effort they might expend using your Web site. It takes the average person only fourteen seconds to decide if a Web page is any good. The good news is that audiences can be moved to

Figure 4.1 The Audience Quadrant.

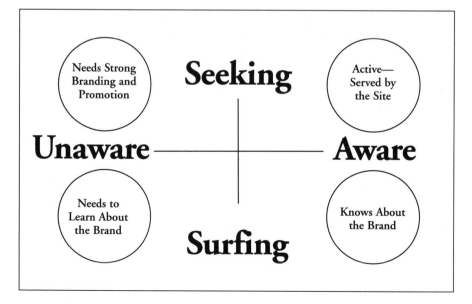

the upper right-hand quadrant very quickly. In 1998, Intel had no e-commerce business; in 1999, they did more than $1 billion a month.[1]

The unaware seeker—the person who wants to buy luggage online but has no idea from whom to buy it—will not type in your uniform resource locator, or URL. So how do you get him or her to your site? By conducting an enormous marketing campaign—but not necessarily using traditional methods. Interactive marketing strategies have proved to be most successful in this endeavor. A luggage manufacturer, for example, might pay for a link at travelocity.com.

Amazon.com is the king of aggressive branding and promotion on the Web. Their name does not suggest books, so how is their awareness so spectacular? In a word, they're everywhere. When you search Yahoo.com, you are offered a direct link to the same search of Amazon.com titles. They've established unusual partnerships with content-oriented sites. In fact, through their affiliate program, any Web site can be a sales channel and provide direct links to recommended titles. In 1999, 65 percent of Amazon.com customers were repeat buyers.

Aware Audiences

As the audience becomes more aware, your site should provide less "who we are" and more functional content. Northwest Airlines is doing a great job with this effort. Its site is so focused on functionality (buying tickets) that the company isn't even talked about.

In order to make the transition from an "aware but surfing" audience to an "aware and seeking" audience, you will need to provide an overall brand that works well both online and offline. You need to establish the Web site as an integral part of your business. This undertaking may require some pretty serious marketing.

United Parcel Service (UPS) is (according to their Web site) the number-one ground shipping company, but no one thought of them as an online company. They tried a consumer-focused strategy to increase awareness of their Web site, but it didn't work. Finally, they went after other e-businesses. UPS made a deal with these sites that allowed them to actually provide site content—interactive package tracking tools—in exchange for using UPS as their shipper. It worked. Now UPS is the e-commerce shipper of choice.

Multiple Audiences, Multiple Services

You've performed your audience analysis, but what if you have more than one audience? How can you build a site that will meet everyone's needs? The answer is you probably can't (or shouldn't), if the customer profiles are significantly different or if your product offerings are distinct.

Time Warner learned this fact the hard way. They defined their audience as the readers of all their publications—*Time, People, Life, Sports Illustrated*, and so on. They created Pathfinder, a Web portal to their multiple brands. As you might guess, this audience definition was not very specific. There is not a particularly large overlap between the readers of *Sports Illustrated*, for example, and *People*. A lack of understanding that each media property has a distinct, and often nonoverlapping, audience was a key factor in the demise of Pathfinder. An individual might log on through the portal to search for sports statistics. Even if that person were also a *People* subscriber, at the moment the user logged on to the Web site, she or he would not want to be distracted by the latest photos of the Princess Di crash scene. Eventually, Time Warner resegmented their audience—but not until they had sunk $170 million into Pathfinder.[2]

The important lesson is that successful companies become what their customers want them to be. You need to create your Web site with this fact in mind. For example, a company might have two audiences that both need product specifications. Business partners need them in order to build the product and customers may need specifications in order to incorporate the product into their final design. Even though they both need the same information, they may need to see it in very different ways. A successful company will recognize this fact and will design electronic businesses to meet these needs.

Yahoo! has done an excellent job of segmenting audiences. They have an all-purpose reception desk in www.yahoo.com. You can use this as a gateway to their many other services, or you can go directly to the other services. For example, audiences with needs for a financial analysis site can go directly to finance.yahoo.com. The site finance.yahoo.com maintains a consistent Yahoo! branding, but it has a different look and feel from the main Yahoo.com Web site. Yahoo! has also built a site for another specific target audience. TV buffs can go to tv.yahoo.com for complete local TV listings. Yahoo! recognizes that its multiple services need distinct treatment.

New Audiences and Opportunities

The Internet provides a myriad of new business opportunities—new audiences that were difficult to market to before, new relationships with current audiences, and opportunities for nontraditional business partnerships. Many successful companies have been surprised to see these opportunities arise. But you can prepare yourself for some of them now.

The biggest change in audience in recent years is in the international market. For example, one of the largest non-American audiences for American Web sites is in Japan. If you examine your Web server log files, you will see that Web users from Japan consistently rate in the top ten countries visiting a Web site. Should you create a Web site for the Japanese market? Many companies have been surprised by the need to incorporate overseas markets into their business plan. FedEx was not an international shipper when it first established a Web page. At that time, DHL had the international market. But FedEx kept getting e-mails from customers asking where its international rates were listed. It had no international rates! Of course, customer demand changed FedEx's business plan dramatically.

Another example of the need to plan for new audiences is in the radio business. Today, radio stations can be accessed over the Internet. They are no longer for local markets only. This larger market has provided a new business opportunity. An entrepreneur now provides a service that inserts national commercials during the time when local commercials are played. The entrepreneur provides a service, and the radio station can double its revenue during those commercial segments.

New relationships with existing audiences are

another new opportunity. Today, audiences actually provide the content for a number of sites. iVillage (www.ivillage.com) is an excellent example. They established their site with the idea of building content for communities of women and families but found that they were too small to be profitable providing their own content. Fortunately, they were able to get their audience to provide the content. iVillage's appeal comes from building, moderating, and promoting discussion forums. Their first success was parenting topics—everyone wants to talk about their kids.

Finally, the Internet provides wonderful new opportunities to create business partnerships that might never have occurred otherwise. I already discussed how UPS provides content for a myriad of e-commerce sites. *The New York Times Book Review* online has direct links that users can utilize to purchase the books from Barnes & Noble. There are many Web portal partnerships—Web sites that are nothing more than bits and pieces of other sites.

Summary

After reading in this chapter about the experiences with building and targeting an audience for a Web site, you should be able to provide a full audience definition for your own Web site.

Figure 4.2 Full Audience Definition.

➤ Primary Audience: Current Customers
  • Home based modem users
  • Already using our products and services
  • Will use the site primarily as a customer service point
➤ Secondary Audience: Potential Customers
  • Home based modem users
  • Seeking information about products and services
  • Want sales follow-up
➤ Tertiary Audience: Investors
  • Seeking information not readily available on standard investing information site, e.g. Annual Report
  • Basic information about the corporation, mission, and officers

---

Figure 4.2 provides an example of a full audience definition. It should provide a detailed account of the characteristics of the primary valued subset, but it should also recognize the other audiences you hope to attract to the site. You may have to do this for multiple audiences or multiple services, if you have distinct sets of valued customers. You will want to limit your offerings to those valued by your audience, so you may need to create more than one Web site. Remember, your e-business exists solely for the benefit of your valued audience.

5

CULTURAL PLANNING

Introduction

Whether you like it or not, computer systems
have changed our way of doing business. You
know a 911 call center has to be up and running
twenty-four hours a day, but does a brokerage
house? In today's economy, the answer is a

resounding yes. There is always a stock market open and a client wanting to make a trade somewhere in the world.

Not only do these companies need to be "open" twenty-four hours a day, but they need to run in real time. Real-time communications means no delays—not for batch processes, not for searching through paperwork. Real-time communications is a one-on-one exchange of information with the customer—now.

The Real-Time Culture

Imagine you're a busy corporate executive booked on a 10:00 a.m. flight to London. You had to attend a meeting before the flight, so you're running for the plane at 9:30. You head straight for the gate, hand the attendant your ticket, and board the plane. Or do you? You see, the attendant doesn't trust a piece of paper—the ticket. He or she trusts the computer system. That is where the most accurate information can be found.

The gate agent must check you in and input data from your ticket that verifies your information in the far more up-to-date computer system. The computer system is where the real work gets done, not the paper ticket. The ticket merely acts as a portable placeholder of information; it tells the agent which keys to hit to verify your status.

This is the key component of a real-time culture: The company puts final trust in the computer system over the words written on a piece of paper. Out of necessity, airlines operate in a real-time environment. So do hotels, CNN, rental car companies, Federal Express, and Amazon.com. Their business relies on technology and their employees are willing to trust the technology precisely because it does not fail them. Therefore, the emphasis on technology reinforces a corporate culture that is conducive to real-time operations. Employees trust that when an item is input into the system, there won't be any part of the company that doesn't know it.

The following four characteristics bring a company into a real-time culture:

1. Where business is done, technology is essential
2. The system is the workflow
3. Employees have a high degree of comfort with computers
4. The company continuously dedicates resources to system development and management

Technology Is Essential

How well can you get your work done without technology? If you can do your job efficiently without technology, there is little incentive to keep the technology up to date. If there are parts of your company with extensive manual work-arounds, employees will not trust the system. They will trust printed reports instead. If your employees don't trust the system (especially if the system really isn't trustworthy), your Web site users won't trust it either. This lack of trust makes it nearly impossible to conduct electronic commerce.

System Is the Workflow

This characteristic is not quite as obvious as the other three. Figure 5.1 presents us with a diagram of a corporation that separates the business into three parts: interface, workflow, and technology.

The interface is those actions that are transparent to the customer. In our airline example, it would be the gate agent and the computer terminal. In an electronic company, that interface might be the Web browser, e-mail, or streaming media. The interface interacts with the workflow on the customer's behalf.

The workflow is how things are done and information is accessed. In the airline example, the

Figure 5.1 Technology and Corporate Culture.

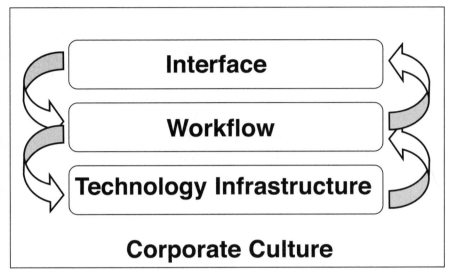

workflow is in the computer system itself. In a traditional environment, that workflow might be the physical manufacture of goods.

Technology provides the support system for both the interface and the workflow. But in a real-time environment, technology does not play a mere supporting role. The technology becomes the workflow itself.

Why does it? Because the workflow is transparent to the customer. Possibly the most innovative feature of the whole Amazon.com process is what the customer does not see—the actual order fulfillment process. If a customer orders a book from Amazon.com, a myriad of tasks must be accomplished to get the book to the customer. The millions of titles in the Amazon.com database are not maintained in a single warehouse. In fact, most of the Amazon.com inventory is not even held by the company. It has a facility in Delaware to fulfill orders, and that facility keeps a collection of best-sellers and frequently purchased titles. However, the company's orders are often filled out of a backlist of titles from the publisher. The Web servers and Web sites unify the disparate technical systems required to manage the workflow so the customer sees only the ordering and receipt of the book.

Many companies view the Web site as just one more separate technology, but Figure 5.2 demonstrates how the Web site can actually become a unifying factor for disparate systems. This function lends itself quite nicely to the creation of a real-time culture. It allows employees to focus on the task at hand rather than the technical aspects of running a business.

High Employee Technology Comfort

Although it may seem obvious to have employees be comfortable with technology, that isn't reality in many corporations. You cannot have a corporate culture that supports a real-time environment if your employees are resistant. Later in this chapter I will go into more detail about how

Figure 5.2 Unifying Technological Infrastructure.

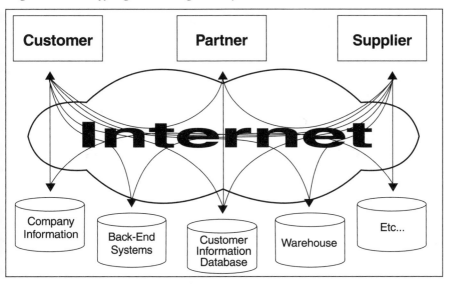

to overcome specific cultural problems, but for now suffice it to say that computers should be everywhere in the company. There are many ways for employees to interface with the system—Web sites, kiosks, scanners, and so on. Even the mailroom should be part of the system.

System Development and Management Resources

Employees will trust the system if the system is trustworthy. So you need to put the time and money into developing a system that works for your business. You also need to encourage your employees to continuously update the system so that it always has the most accurate and up-to-

date information. The entire day-to-day workflow should revolve around keeping the system
up to date.

Effecting a Culture Shift

Corporate culture can thwart the best efforts at
creating an electronic organization. If, for what-
ever reason, your company is not ready to trust
the system, there is little sense in jumping into
an e-commerce initiative full-force. You must
address cultural issues in the first phases of moving toward real time.

Decision Makers

You (or your manager) may have entered the
workforce when computers were big machines in
locked rooms and typing was for secretaries.
Business has been good for the last twenty years.
And you didn't need the Internet to get where
you are today. In fact, neither did Donald
Trump, Warren Buffett, or Lee Iacocca. So why
do you need to learn this stuff now?

Because you are selling to customers who understand technology. Because you are competing
against people who understand technology.
Because the Internet is here to stay.

Even so, it can be very hard to get a decision

maker who made her or his money "the old-fashioned way" to recognize the importance of understanding technology. The single biggest challenge to many electronic commerce initiatives is the prejudices of the upper executives.

Ideally, you would change those prejudices. But often that is not a practical solution. You probably won't be able to get them to go online. It typically would take too much time; meanwhile, your company would be falling further and further behind.

If you can't work with executives who are comfortable with technology, be sure your e-business plans emphasize business results. Don't talk about the technology. Don't show them Web site prototypes. Don't even talk about the functional benefit to customers. Instead, talk strictly numbers—cost avoidance, increased sales, cost savings, and so on. This should get you your executive buy-in.

The Sales Team

Interestingly enough, the second most common cultural barrier can be found in the sales force. Salespeople don't like the idea of losing contact with their customers. They're afraid they'll be replaced by an electronic order-taking process. They see the Web site as a competitor.

The ironic part is that a well-crafted Web site can actually have a positive effect on the sales force. In many ways, today's salespeople have become little more than order takers. With the push to get more work done with fewer people, very little consultative selling is actually done these days.

The Internet can free the salespeople to do that consultative selling, instead of data entry. Furthermore, the Internet can add value to the customer relationship by putting the sales force everywhere the customer is. Of course, the exact effect of e-business on your sales force will depend on the nature of the buying decision in your market. But here are some examples of effective uses of the Internet that might help you get started thinking about how to bring the sales force along.

There is an electronics store in New York City called J&R Music World. It has always had telephone and catalog sales, but it also has a commissioned sales force on the floor. Why? The salespeople act as consultants. They understand the equipment and can assist customers in the buying process. J&R Music World discovered that many of its customers were coming into the shop to view the equipment and speak with a salesperson and would buy the system online later. The reason was simple—the buying decision is often one that customers like to spend some time on. They like to discuss it with a spouse, comparison shop, or simply mull it over. The sales force wasn't happy when they lost the commission after putting time into a consultation, but the company realized the need to give customers the ability to buy electronics when they make up their minds, even if that is at 2:00 a.m. Today, when salespeople consult on a sound system, they can hand customers a business card with a salesperson number on it next to the Web site address. That way, customers are encouraged to make the purchase in the fashion most convenient for them, and a salesperson still gets a commission when the salesperson number is entered along with the Internet order.

My Solomon Smith Barney broker is there to build a relationship with me. Sometimes I need his help, and I'm glad I can call on him. Often I don't. The functionality of the Web site actually solidifies the relationship I have with Solomon Smith Barney because I know I can count on the company to be there when I need it. My broker can take more time with me personally when I need consultation because he's not taking a thousand little orders. And I can complete simple transactions online any time of day or night.

The car buying process is a complex mixture of an informational sell and an emotional sell.

When Subaru made their first foray into e-commerce, their dealerships were not happy about it. They felt they were losing the opportunity to sell to customers one on one. What they found instead was that the customers who visited the site before coming in for a test drive had a much higher probability of completing a sale. These customers already knew the facts and figures about the car and were already "sold" on the statistics. Now the salesperson could focus in on emotional sell, which is typically what career salespeople enjoy most.

Operational Employees

Your operational employees—the people who make your business work—can pose quite a threat to e-commerce if they're not ready to participate. There are three basic reasons your employees might not trust the system:

1. Bad experiences with technology
2. Fear of being displaced
3. Lack of education

Bad Experiences With Technology. Employees often have had bad experiences with technology when there are bad processes in the company. It's important to remember that no one will trust a system that's not trustworthy. You have to get your house in order before you can expect your employees to rely on the system. Even then, it may take a while for the system to "prove" itself.

I was recently charged with designing e-commerce for a company that sells wholesale goods to restaurants. I sold them on the idea of hooking up the Web page to their internal system so that orders would flow directly into the system without intervention. When I asked the important question, "How do you want the data formatted?" They looked at me blankly. You see, they didn't have the means of connecting the data because they had been manually working around broken systems. They had staff members entering data into the system from bits of paper that carried the day's corrections. Management was not fully aware of the problem. Several employees had proposed a change to the system a few years before, but they had abandoned the proposal when it was obvious there was little buy-in. These broken systems were exposed when employees tried to hook the Internet orders directly into the inventory system. This story has a happy ending. I was able to take the original proposal for system fixes and re-present it to management. The employees who had originally worked on the proposal were given the credit, and the system had immediate buy-in.

Fear of Being Displaced. Fortunately, the fear of being displaced by technology is mostly unfounded today. Most companies are already working on such low staffs anyway that employees can be moved to fill other needs. Everybody wins in these situations. The company makes better use of its staff—higher operational efficiencies and less burnout. And the employees are typically more satisfied with their jobs because they are now doing something more meaningful.

Lack of Education. For most people, a computer is nothing more than a word processor and an e-mail machine. Very few understand the true power of a computer.

Training is the obvious solution, yet most companies simply don't give it much emphasis. Jeff Bezos, founder and CEO of Amazon.com, once said that "if football teams trained the way most companies trained, they'd all get together Saturday night for one half hour before the Sunday game."

Many companies object to extensive training because they fear that employees will leave them and take the skill set with them. Of course this will happen to some extent, but that's the price of doing business. You simply can't function as a company with an untrained workforce. To build a real-time culture, everyone needs computer skills, even receptionists.

Find the training style that works best for your company and your workforce. Training can be in the form of mentoring or it can be classroom style. There are conferences and hands-on workshops. The point is, any training is better than nothing. A single class in how to do research on the Internet would do more good for most administrative assistants than fifty hours of stumbling around.

In the world of little training, there are some excellent examples of corporations that have taken innovative approaches to training their employees in technology.

In 1999, Tandy Corporation installed Web terminals in warehouses expressly for their employees to use to go shopping on the Internet while on their breaks. Their reasoning: If we're going to sell online, we want our employees to understand what our customers are doing.

Ford Motor Company and Delta Airlines have both instituted low- or no-cost computers and Internet access for employees to take home. This setup allows the employees to become comfortable with computers in a nonthreatening environment.

Bloomberg, the financial services company, sends employees for several months of paid training. It can be a hard place to work, so people are trained with the tools they'll need to work there. The company administers tests and performance assessments. When trainees finish up, they really know Bloomberg products and services.

◼ Summary

Have you ever called a company and gotten a recording that said, "please call us back during normal business hours"? What are normal business hours? Over the last century, we have established a routine of going to the office, doing our work, and coming home—all at prescribed times.

But the Internet is changing our perception of a "normal" workweek. "Normal" is now when the customer wants to do business. And the customer usually wants to do business "now."

In Chapter 1, I discussed an inherent internationalization of commerce with the Internet. If you have the technology, people will want to do business with you on a global basis. This is one more push on the need to be open twenty-four hours. Differences in time zones mean that somebody is always awake and wanting to do business. Right now I am working with a colleague in London. At 2:00 p.m. my time, he's getting ready to go to bed. But I've still got quite a number of good hours left in the day. I can pick up on the project where he left off, and he'll have my work by the time he wakes up the next morning. The concept of time zones has gotten so ridiculous in this Internet age that CNN.com has started posting time in "Internet time." Each day is divided into 1,000 beats, which are the same no matter what time zone you are living in.

Recent pushes toward flex time and telecommuting—both of which are facilitated by technology changes—actually make a real-time organization a possibility. The spreading out of the workforce across times is, in many respects, a shift back to the patterns of an agrarian society that worked when there was work to be done. Of course, you will still need to schedule meetings. But a 2:00 p.m. meeting can be the start of the workday for some and the end of the workday for others.

This cultural shift requiring a real-time organization is inevitable. The successful implementation of a real-time organization, though, depends on a culture that is comfortable with technology and is willing to rely on the system over paper documents.

6

THE INFOSTRUCTURE

Introduction

Imagine your company makes electronic widgets, and you typically sell 100 at a time. One day, you get an e-mail message from an existing customer asking the following:

I'd like to purchase a large quantity (11,000 pieces) of your model 245 widget; however, I need them to be modified to operate on 220 volts. It is imperative I get a time and cost estimate on this order quickly. I will be traveling from New York to London today; however, I plan to check my e-mail when I land in London, about seven hours from now. I'll expect relevant information by then.

How would your company handle this request? Would it go to sales first? Or would it go to engineering? Who authors the response?

In Chapter 1, I introduced the concept of the infostructure. As the name implies, the infostructure is the organization of information within your corporation, and it establishes an ownership of information necessary for authoritative dissemination of information to the outside world. Though difficult, the infostructuring process is necessary to clearly define electronic communications channels that center on customer needs and expectations.

If information is managed properly, there is actually no need for an organizational chart. The Gore Company (makers of Gore-Tex®) has no job titles. New employees are sent to work with teams based on their skill sets—but they don't know what those teams will be in advance. This is not a small company. This is a $4.2 billion company.

Creating the Master Information Map

The first step to designing an effective infostructure is to create a master information map. This map represents the way the audience interacts with information in your organization. It is fundamentally different from your organizational chart because it is based on how your primary audience expects your company to work for them, not how it is actually structured.

To begin an infostructure process, start by listing all the content or information that the public may access. Then, group this content based on its interrelationship to audience needs (not your organizational structure).

For an idea of how the process might work for a hypothetical widget-selling organization, refer to Figure 6.1, which presents a list of potential content items. Obviously, this list is far shorter and simpler than a real list of content areas of a Web site.

Figure 6.1 Hypothetical Content List for Widget Manufacturer.

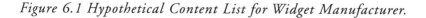

Product Specifications
Product Sell Sheets
Pictures of Products
Engineering Drawings of Products
Secure Order Form
About the Company
Company Contact Information
Dealer List
Product Support Information

In a company-centric approach, it is common to see content lists, as shown in Figure 6.2. This approach is an all-too-common one, and it leads to end-user frustration. For example, product support is really a logical extension of product information. Why should a customer have to exit one area to get to the other? Also, different customer segments may have completely different needs. In this example, the product information is completely unsegmented.

When infostructuring, you need to think about how a customer might expect to use your site. So structure the site around customer usage. Thus, you would have a different interface structure such as that found in Figure 6.3. (Note that in the figure only "Industrial" is fully mapped out.) This seemingly simple change in sequence makes

Figure 6.2 Company-Centric Content Groupings for Widget Manufacturer.

Products	Support	Company
Product List (Alphabetical list of Product Sell Sheets & Product Pictures)	Product Support Pages	"About the Company"
Engineering Drawings of Products	Contact Support	Company Contact Information
Dealers Online Ordering		

a substantial difference in the way the end user works with the site.

After infostructuring is done, develop a visual map of the logical groupings. This map will reflect where the information is found, even when the same information can be found or used in multiple places.

Identify Key People and Systems

For each content piece, you will want to identify people and systems that are key to the deployment of the information. All organizations have a chain of ownership for all information. There are three types of people and systems that should be identified now: information authorities, information sources, and implementers. Figure 6.4 graphically illustrates their relationship.

Information authorities are the people who are ultimately responsible for the information. They

Figure 6.3 Customer-Centric Infostructure Approach.

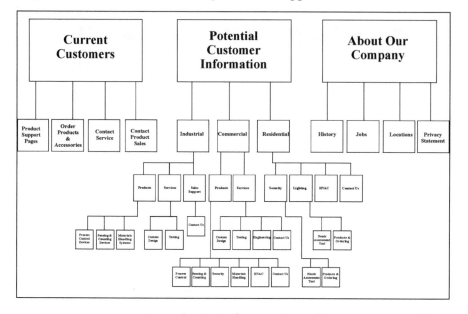

may receive their information from sources, but they are the owners of that information. For example, a sales forecast is ostensibly issued by a department (for example, accounting or sales), but some individual within the department is the ultimate authority over what goes into the forecast, how it is presented to the company, and so on. Without an owner, a project simply cannot continue.

Sources are people or systems that provide some sort of useful information to the information authority. Going back to our sales forecast example, each member of the sales force might act as a source by providing individual projections of

Figure 6.4 Key People and Systems.

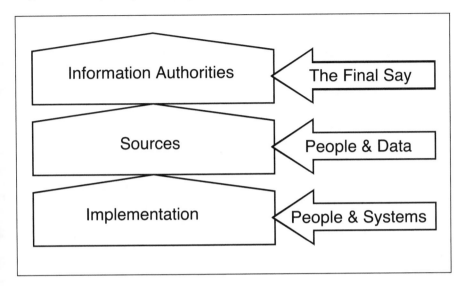

sales in their territory. The database of past sales might also serve as a source for the information authority who then analyzes all the information gathered for the final report. Information sources may also be information implementers.

Implementers are the people or systems that are responsible for the actual creation, dissemination, entry, and manipulation of information gathered by sources and sent out by the owners. These are the database administrators, programmers, data entry clerks, administrative assistants, analysts, and others who do the work of creating documents and information. These people are crucial to the success of any project, even if they are organizationally at a much lower level than the information authority or information source.

Electronic Opportunities for Information Flow

If your company is like most, your information map for an individual project now looks a lot like Figure 6.5. You've identified a group of sources that forward information to a group of analysts (implementers) who consolidate and interpret the data. That data is then sent to the information authority for approval and then to the final group of implementers who print, fax, and broadcast the report. Although this flow of information gets the job done, it is tedious.

Many companies are automating the implementer stages (see Figure 6.6) to speed up the process. The sources now provide information directly to a system that consolidates the information electronically and forwards it in the form of an e-mail to the information authority. The approval of the information authority triggers an automatic electronic publishing of the material. Although this is an excellent improvement over the first scenario, it does not fundamentally alter the steps in the process—it only automates them.

A company that can think outside of the traditional information flow will see there is no reason for these steps at all. The sources can create

Figure 6.5 Current State Information Flow.

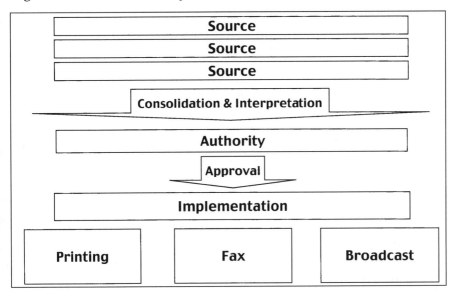

Figure 6.6 Information Flow: Automated Implementation.

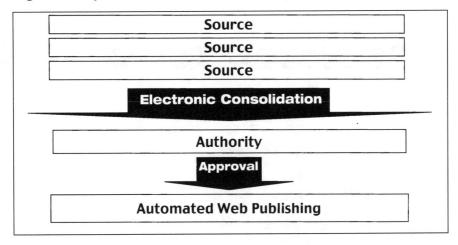

the document in the initial pass using Web-page tools in a group publishing environment. All that is necessary is for the information authority to monitor the sources (see Figure 6.7).

Your sales forecast can be published on an intranet without intermediate steps. The sales force can enter the data directly and the computer system can automatically post an updated report.

I'll expand on the practical aspects of group publishing in Chapter 8, but suffice it to say, group publishing allows the information flow to be equivalent to the workflow. There is no translation needed.

Figure 6.7 Direct Information Flow.

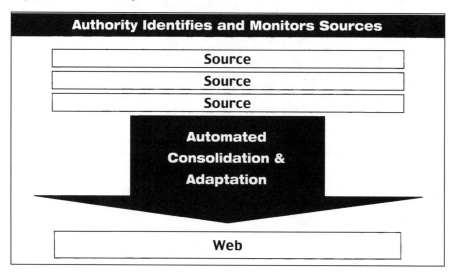

New Information Map for Customer Response

Customers are tired of being put on hold by an automated customer service system. For nonurgent but important communications, customers are realizing that an e-mail message to a company eliminates the time-wasting burden of waiting on the phone for answers to questions they need *soon* but not *now*. However, although consumers see e-mail as a quick way to open up an efficient communications channel, companies are faced with a new challenge: managing an effective response. In most organizations, e-mail messages bypass the normal customer service structures. There is very little control over the responses. E-mail messages may go unanswered, or worse, answered with the wrong information from the wrong part of the company.

But corporations also like e-mail as a form of communication. It provides significant cost savings and, if handled properly, can be a better medium for providing a high level of service.

Remember the example of the request for modified widgets at the beginning of this chapter? The problem this request presents is that the information touches several different departments in a traditional company. Sales will want to get involved in the pricing issue; engineering will need to make estimates due to design changes; and production will have to schedule the plant time. So how do you approach it when there could be an information authority in each department?

Having multiple information authorities creates "information islands." These are perfectly good and useful pieces of information that are not communicated properly to the rest of the organization. This poor communication can result in pockets of information that are completely out of synch with the rest of the organization. You must find and eliminate these islands. If your "current state" information map has multiple information authorities for a particular piece of information, now is the time to narrow that to a single authority. Each department will still be involved in the response—but as providers or sources of information.

Response Management

First and foremost, you want to make sure all incoming e-mail messages are responded to by the right person in a timely fashion. Now that you've assigned information authorities for each piece of content, building a routing table for incoming e-mail should be relatively easy.

Fairly common questions should be routed to

implementers for predesigned responses, but any new or unique e-mail message should be routed directly to the information authority. You might want to forward a copy to the identified sources simultaneously to facilitate communication among the information authority and the sources. The information authority will take responsibility for the response.

If you have a high volume of customer communication, you might want to integrate e-mail handling with your current customer service call center. Although these projects can have a high initial outlay to develop, they can provide a good return on investment by lowering telecommunications costs and increasing the efficiency of the customer service staff.

Finally, you will want to use e-mail response analysis as a basis for Web site improvement planning. Customers frequently will e-mail a company because the information on the Web site did not meet their needs or was too hard to find. Although e-mail response is considerably less expensive than traditional customer service, it still is more expensive than self-directed customer service through a good Web service. Archiving and analyzing the e-mail communications over time will help to identify unmet customer needs and is a valuable part of the Web site planning process.

▪▪▪▪ Summary

In the electronic economy, customers expect speed, but not at the expense of accuracy. Every customer is hoping your Web site will provide them with the information they are seeking, but if it doesn't, they expect you to be able to answer their questions in a timely fashion. Unfortunately, few companies have set up efficient information flows that allow for this kind of response.

An infostructure will help you attack this issue aggressively. First, a good information authority will monitor sources of information to be sure the most accurate, complete, and updated information is published on your Web site. Not only will this effort make for happier customers, it will generate cost savings if customers have fewer questions.

Of course, questions or unique situations will arise. At such times the infostructure is really allowed to shine, by providing a map for obtaining the necessary information and establishing a responsible party that won't allow a request to slip through the cracks.

7

BUILDING
THE INITIAL
WEB SITE

Introduction

This is the chapter where we get down to business. To this point, I've tried to steer away from too much technical and operational detail in favor of communicating to you the importance of a strategic approach to the Web site. If you haven't figured out the urgency of creating a corporate culture that can effectively operate in real time and the necessity of strategic direction for any e-business activities, go back and reread Chapters 1 to 6. But if you're ready to build—or do a major overhaul—read on.

The Interactive Council

Online, organizations have a single interface (the computer screen) with which they will present the whole company. But most organizations today are fractionalized internally. Yet the concerns of the brand manager are just as valid as those of the information technology (IT) department. How do you coordinate the technical, communications, operational, sales, branding, and marketing aspects of a Web site?

By creating an interactive council made up of key stakeholders, you can coordinate any Web development initiative as well as the continuing maintenance and improvement of the Web site. The council will identify, propose, evaluate, and develop important e-business opportunities.

The formation of an interactive council is done to ensure that, online at least, the company presents a unified front and coordinates efforts to create an experience for the customer that is consistent, predictable, and highly functional.

The interactive council should be kept to a maximum of twenty active participants at any given time. There are six primary roles that should be represented in the council:

1. A coordinating member (e-business manager)
2. Decision owners (not evaluators) from sales, operations, and information systems
3. Rotating day-to-day management representation from sales and/or marketing and operations
4. A representative from the outsourcing firm, if part of the process is outsourced
5. Representatives from the design and technical groups, if development is done in-house
6. A representative from an ad agency, if one is used

E-Business Manager

The e-business manager's role was at one time called the "Web master." This role has evolved from the person responsible for executing the delivery of all online activities to the person responsible for integrating cross-functional communications and executing the planning necessary for effective interactive communications.

It is the responsibility of the e-business manager to coordinate the interactive development efforts throughout the company, expanding on good "renegade" ideas that spring up and squelching projects that are off the mark. Additionally, the e-business manager of the interactive council acts to facilitate communications between business silos and to introduce new ideas for interactive business capabilities to the group.

The e-business manager will also act to solicit and select vendors necessary to assist in development and deployment of interactive capabilities. Ultimately, the e-business manager role is referee within the company and advocate for the customer experience.

Decision Owners

Decision owners are quite possibly the most vital part of the interactive council. Decision *owners* are very different from decision makers. A decision owner does more than make decisions; she or he answers to nobody else, has final budget authority, and can effect change within her or his functional area by mandate, if necessary. For example, a decision owner from an engineering group would be able to say for certain whether or not a standard product specification sheet was effective for use online.

The need for decision owners from specific disciplines will vary by company, but typically the council will want a decision owner from sales and marketing, operations (for example, accounting, shipping, or human resources), and information systems.

Day-to-Day Management

Day-to-day management may or may not overlap with the decision owners. If not, it is critical to include them in the ongoing planning or analysis of interactive efforts. For example, the head of human resources (a decision owner) may sit on the council. He or she would be the one to make the final decision to create an online résumé form. But only the people who review the online résumés on a daily basis will be able to determine what improvements may be needed, and they need a forum in which to communicate their needs.

Outsource Representative

Many organizations seek to outsource a portion of key interactive projects. It is essential that the outsource company be given a seat on the council to ensure that its employees are able to understand all aspects of their assigned projects and to be able to raise and resolve issues quickly.

In-House Development Group

Like the outside developer, any internal development groups need routine participation in the council meetings. This is especially important for technical developers, such as programmers and networking specialists. They are closest to the real work of the company and will add great value to the council.

Ad Agency Representation

If your organization is using an advertising agency (or has an in-house group acting in that role) it is very important to ensure that representatives from that agency are regular participants in all meetings. This representation will help to ensure consistent brand messaging, will keep the agency in the loop about new opportunities for promotion and advertising, and will enable the council to remain apprised of new campaigns and plans that might require changes to the online service.

Interactive Council Activities

The interactive council will be at their busiest during the initial development of the Web site. They should not meet physically very often. The council should be able to use interactive communications tools (such as eGroups.com) to coordinate efforts. If not, they will waste quite a bit of time. Of course, the council will also be responsible for overseeing the maintenance of the site and the improvement of the site over time. In this function, they should meet face to face at least quarterly.

Any active member of the council can propose new interactive projects or revisions to existing efforts. The e-business manager consolidates the proposals and brings them to "meetings" (electronic or in person), which are used to present ideas in a neutral context for evaluation and cross-functional planning.

These meetings also serve as a cross-functional planning session for projects that are underway. Results of ongoing projects can be assessed and continued or canceled as needed.

Staffing for Web Site Development

Although it is impossible to define all the roles that will work for each organization, there is a fairly simple defined set of needs that all interactive development projects have. These roles are not independent of one another. Rather, they represent a team of people who need to continually check what they are doing against one another's work.

Any of these roles can be performed by in-house staff or outsourced as needed. When a global project is undertaken, the roles are taken on by local hires who execute tasks under the guidance of the global interactive council. Depending on the size of the effort, these roles may eventually be performed by departments with their own staffing. In all cases, each of these roles comes under the direction (direct where possible) of the e-business manager of the interactive council, who tasks them with the appropriate strategic projects.

Information Architect

The information architect is the user advocate and as such is also the team leader. She or he best understands the ultimate goal of the project. It is that person's job to ensure that the user experience is *consistent* and *predictable*. The information architect is concerned with the "flow" of the user interaction and analyzes the various ways that the online service will be used. He or she develops functional maps and flowcharts and identifies needs for conceptual, technical, or visual improvements.

The information architect seeks to develop a library of interaction methods that are used consistently in the project. For example, a search function must have a clear way of collecting search terms, formatting and delivering results, and handling "exceptions" in the event of an error. This functional need is coordinated with technical requirements, such as the kinds of data to be searched, the syntax of the search terms, and so on. The information architect works closely with the writer, graphic designer, and interface builder to coordinate messaging and presentation prior to final interface development. The information architect is an important part of the interactive council.

Graphic Designer/Visual Director

The graphic designer is responsible for creating the online visual library. This material includes iconography, screen layouts [as validated by the interface builder (see below)], and related visual design elements. The graphic designer will ensure that the online representation of the corporate "look" is carried through to the online user experience. This effort does not necessarily mean duplicating the existing visual library of a company; in fact, it often involves creating an appropriate online extension of the company's visual elements. The graphic designer works closely with the interface builder and information architect in developing user interfaces. The graphic designer's job is ultimately to make sure that a picture is really worth a thousand words.

Writer

The writer is responsible for developing functional copy that best fits the needs of the interactive environment. Writing online is not top to bottom, left to right. Online writing takes the form of "information nuggets." The online writer will understand the "third dimension" of interactive communications: writing for navigation. This task includes the integration of pull-down menus, hyperlink, "rollover" text, and so on in a format that is intuitive to the user.

Adam.com is a medical reference encyclopedia that makes pieces of writing as useful as the links between them. Rather than use the traditional page to explain every last detail, Adam.com describes only what is unique at that point and uses hyperlinks to complete the thought. It is a digestible interlinked network of concepts rather than a traditional essay.

The writer works closely with the information architect (sometimes they are the same person) and the interface builder. The writer's goal is to use words as efficiently as possible and to allow interactivity to assist in the message delivery.

Interface Builder

The interface builder is concerned with constructing the code that is sent to the user's computer to build a screen and provide interaction. The code involves everything from basic HTML page development to sophisticated JavaScript, Cascading Style Sheets, ActiveX controls, and much more. Most important, the interface builder needs to learn how to construct scalable interfaces for wireless devices, hand-held computers, and kiosks. Thus, interface development becomes a complex suite of technical and design challenges.

Server Programmer

Server programming is especially important when the user interface includes lots of interactive capabilities, connects to legacy systems (such as mainframes, minicomputers like the IBM AS/400, and similar "old" systems), or has Web server side database programming. This role takes care of programs that reside on the Web server itself or are used to access other systems. Skills in this role would include Perl scripting and perhaps some C or C++.

Server Administrator

The role of server administrator is concerned with maintaining the operating system, server software, security, network connections, and other aspects of keeping the Web server online. The server administrator is not concerned with custom programming, content, or any other aspects of the Web server.

Network Integrator

The network integrator will come from your information technology group. This role is a coordinating role. The network integrator is also responsible for software selection and authoring for the "middleware" that is used to connect Web servers to other systems on the network. For example, the network integrator might be needed to ensure that the appropriate software and systems are installed to facilitate the integration of a Web-based order status checking system. The network integrator works closely with the server programmer and server administrator.

Quality Assurance

Quality assurance (QA) is a user-experience-testing role. Like any software, Web services need continual testing and monitoring for potential errors ranging from typographical errors in the copy to server failures. During development, the QA role conducts cross-platform testing to ensure a consistent user experience. The QA continually checks the end product of the production group and also monitors site performance and availability.

Outsourcing

Once you've developed a Web strategy, you need to decide what portion of the work you can do in-house and what portion you will outsource. If you were to go to the top Web sites (CyberAtlas.com has a list of this week's top twenty-five), you'd find that they all do a majority of their own work in-house. Even so, many of them outsource major portions of their Web site.

There is no clear directive as to which portion of the work best lends itself to outsourcing. Both eBay and Charles Schwab currently use Razorfish.com to do interface work while they handle the structural portion (e.g., database management) internally. Yahoo! does its own interface and programming but outsources the servers to GlobalConnect.

There are two steps to determining what to outsource. First, you need to do a skills assessment. Can you provide this service in house? Second, you need to look at the issue strategically. Is this an area of strategic importance to your business?

Determining Skills Needed

Before you tackle a Web project, you will want to be sure you have the skills—or can acquire them in a reasonable time frame—to carry out such a project. Look first at your current IT department. How well are they meeting their current goals? Remember, this project will require additional IT time. You can't simply reassign people from maintaining internal networks.

Second, analyze your organization in terms of its readiness to run a 24/7 operation—twenty-four hours a day, seven days a week. Do you have the staffing to take on mission-critical applications in a 24/7 environment? Do you have the type of facility that lends itself to being a 24/7 data center? Do you have the necessary security? You might wish to consider having the service hosted by a third party.

Third, do you have the in-house skills for user-interface design and construction? Remember, the design doesn't involve just visual design (though that's a substantial portion of it). The interface design is an interactive design. The designer decides what happens when you click on something, the type of language structure, the use of pull-down menus, and so on. If you don't have these skills in house, look carefully at your ability to acquire them. Although it is not impossible to hire an interface designer, in most parts of the country, the very best designers tend to migrate to Web design shops.

Finally, you will need to analyze your ability to maintain the Web site internally. Can you reasonably expect your people to update the site themselves? If there is no comfort level with computers currently, you can't expect that installing a Web site will make them more comfortable overnight.

Analyzing Outsource Strategy

Of course, some of the answers to the skills assessment may make you lean toward outsourcing. But before you commit yourself to any long-term outsourcing strategy, you will want to analyze the process from a business strategy angle. Ask yourself, is this part of the process key to my business strategy? If it is, chances are you won't want to outsource it—at least not long term.

One question you might ask is whether or not it makes sense to provide your own server and bandwidth. Perhaps in your business there are a large number of lookers and not many buyers. That would mean a lot of bandwidth you would have to provide from your offices. Is that necessary for your strategic focus? Often the answer would be "no." An outsourcer might be able to provide a server at a much lower cost because of shared services with other companies.

Another example might be an IT department that is barely able to keep up with its own network responsibilities. If potential hires are in short supply, you might want to outsource the initial development of the Web site. But even if you do, that does not mean you won't need Web design skills down the road. You will want to develop them in-house while you are simultaneously using a third party to jump-start your Web page. That way, you will be able to properly maintain and improve your site without depending on your supplier.

Of course, if your analysis leads you to believe the user interface is not the most strategic element of your site (for example, you will not be needing to improve upon it on a regular basis), you may decide you want to outsource this process on a continual basis.

Even if you have continual outsourcing, don't ignore in-house maintenance skills. If you used an outsource company to design interface templates, you would still want to be continually updating and managing the content on the site. If your people are not comfortable updating electronic information, you will need to invest in some training. Do not buy a Web site that you cannot maintain.

It is the role of the e-business manager to determine that any long-term outsourcing is for strategic reasons only, not for reasons of internal incompetence. That person must be sure that the company not only doesn't possess the skill now but also will never need it. For most e-businesses that are outsourcing, the building of the initial site or the bandwidth is what is being outsourced. But information architecture may ultimately be a good candidate for outsourcing as well if your product has complex configuration possibilities. Ultimately, good information architecture is your business, your strategy, and your responsibility. Do buy services to provide stability or to get a jump-start on your Web site, but you must have the skill sets internally to maintain the site long term.

Building the Relationship

There is a long-standing joke that all outsource relationships begin with wild enthusiasm and end with a search for the guilty parties. Try not to let that happen to you. Do not wait to bring in extra help until you've discovered that you have a big problem. Instead, make the decision to go with an outsourcing company part of your strategic approach to e-business.

You will actually save a great deal of money in the long run if you bring in an outside designer, data communications specialist, programmer, or other outsourcing representative when you are planning the strategic approach to the Web site. Yes, you would have to pay them to attend meetings, but the money spent is worth it in the long run. You will need to allocate at least 10 percent of your total project budget just for planning and prototyping (even if you're doing these tasks in-house). Sometimes the figure can get as high as 50 percent. But a good project plan leads to a much better understanding of the project needs and a significantly better product for less money.

Before you ever go to an outsource developer, you need to set a company list of goals for your Web site. Otherwise, you will find yourself playing a game of twenty questions with your developer (and paying him or her for it too). Don't go with just a general desire to get on the Internet.

Be specific. For example, you might say, "We need to reduce cost of sales and we need you to understand our selling process." Don't just say you want something that looks good and is state of the art. Instead, define the business function you want the Web site to achieve. For example, you might want it to load in under twenty seconds and operate on multiple browsers and function on a modem. Otherwise, you might end up with a beautiful Web site that is a monstrosity to load and has no functionality for your customers. If you did the exercise in goal setting in Chapter 3 and the audience definition exercise in Chapter 4, your development efforts no doubt will be successful.

Another hint: If you use an outside design company, you will generally spend a lot of money seeing prototypes you don't like. It will save a lot of money in the planning process if you bring your designer printouts of ten Web sites you like and ten you can't stand. Think about the sites you personally use every day and list reasons you use them. Avoid the temptation to build a slick, glossy site at the expense of functionality. AOL and Yahoo! are consistently ranked as top sites, but they're not slick.

It is your job to make the outsource developer understand your company's philosophy toward the site. For example, if you are outsourcing interface design, you must communicate that you want something customers will love to use—that the site is being built for the customers. Focus the design company on your customers' needs.

Or, if you decided to outsource bandwidth, you will also recognize that slow servers or down servers won't contribute to your goal of increasing sales. So, you will need to discuss your expectations for things like uptime, bandwidth, and response rates with your outsourcer upfront as you develop the initial relationship.

Work out a relationship that allows both you and the developer to contribute your strengths to the project. You know your business best; don't let others tell you what your business is. On the other hand, other professionals might understand interactive technology; let them tell you how interactive technology can help your business. Together you can understand how to do business better.

Finally, make sure the developer is willing to let you operate the content of your own site. If the developer wants to control content and modifications in the future, you will find the site too cumbersome to operate in real time as part of your process. Make sure the developer is willing to construct the interface as a template within which you can maintain content on a day-to-day basis. Remember, your eventual goal is to integrate operations to the point that the workflow is the Web site.

Managing an Ongoing Relationship

If you are going to have an outsource relationship that lasts any length of time, you will need to manage the relationship carefully. As already discussed, the outsource company will have representation on the interactive council, and the e-business manager will have primary responsibility for coordinating with the outsourcer. This relationship means that the outsourcer must be treated as a member of your team, not as a separate company. If the outsourcer will be dealing with sensitive information, you might want to set up noncompetitive or confidentiality agreements in the original contract. But no matter what you decide, outsourcers must be active members of your development team.

The vendor must be allowed to make important contributions to the interactive council. Remember that when you picked the outsource vendor, you did so based on key aspects of your business plan; the vendor was picked because of its relevant competency. The vendor's competencies are essential to your success. For example, a data communications vendor should be able to help you build and operate a mission-critical system, even if your in-house team has never done a project like it. Beware of the vendor who leaves the "heavy lifting" of development to your in-house staff.

Despite their membership on the interactive council, vendors must live up to certain expectations. Be sure to set clear goals at the outset. Then you must continuously measure the vendor's success and update any further expectations. Although it is not their place to set the expectations, many of the best vendors will actually be able to help you set goals, because they are more familiar with the technology.

Don't wait until something major has gone wrong to give your outsource vendors feedback. Of course, if vendors are on your interactive council, they will probably be getting some ongoing feedback—and that's great. But before you wake up mad at everyone, set up definite review dates. There is little sense in having a formal review more often than every three months—but don't go longer than six months without one either. The review should discuss the company's positive contributions, where it needs to improve, and the strategy for making those improvements.

Terminating the Outsource Relationship

Finally, when dealing with an outside vendor,

you need to know when to say it's over. There are three reasons you might terminate a relationship with your outsource vendor. First, the vendor's performance might not be up to par. This fact should become evident as you have your formal quarterly reviews. Second, sometimes the needs of your company simply outgrow the vendor's capabilities. Although this is nobody's "fault," it is important to recognize this possibility so that you can move on. Finally, you might find that you no longer need the vendor because you have developed the competency in-house. Charles Schwab happily found itself in this scenario recently. The company used to outsource the majority of its e-business work. Now, it has improved its internal capabilities and contracts only the user interface and specific special projects.

You will need to do a cost-benefit analysis before deciding to move the operations in-house, but if you can get and retain talent, and it makes strategic sense, then it is time to move on.

Although many procurement operations are tending toward long-term contracts, the interactive world simply moves too quickly for drawing up anything more than an annual contract. Even the Internal Revenue Service has changed its amortization rules such that you can now write off computer equipment in one year. You just don't know where technology will be one year from now or whether your vendor will be able to meet your needs. What would have happened if you had signed a five-year contract with Netscape in 1998? Even though Netscape had one of the most successful initial public offerings in history, it's gone now. No matter how promising a company looks, you simply can't predict far enough in the future to deal with anything more than a one-year contract.

Budgeting for E-Commerce

Whether you decide to do your Web development project in house or use an outsource vendor, it will cost you about the same as a new telephone system. Of course, just like a phone system, the bigger you are or the fancier your system, the more it will cost. The following description should help you set some reasonable expectations for a Web development project.

If you are an average company with 100 employees and one location that is already spending money to maintain a technology infrastructure, expect to spend a minimum of $20,000 for a Web site with basic functionality, reasonable interactivity, and common expectations capabilities. This site would be free-standing and would not be integrated with other technologies in your company.

The same average company that wants a few more e-commerce capabilities such as shopping and catalog management should expect to spend $50,000 to $60,000. Of course, there's a big jump after that. For companies with multiple locations and full integration, Web sites can range from $250,000 to $4 million or $5 million.

Keep in mind that these suggested costs are in addition to the other IT monies you are already spending. You cannot take Web development money from any other budget. In fact, you *must* have a regular budget already in place for maintaining your company's technology. I run into companies all the time that treat technology as a one-time expense and do not budget for regular maintenance and improvement. In modern business, the technology budget should be an annual expense, like the advertising budget, not a one-time cost. As with advertising, if you invest in technology only once and then stop, you will quickly lose business. My budgeting assumption is that your company already has adequate technology to support interactive activities. If this is not the case, the numbers suggested above could be off by as much as 50 percent.

Of course, your company may not be average. Typically, you would need to add 10 to 15 percent for each additional 100 employees and 5 to 10 percent for each additional location you would want to integrate. There might also be geographic requirements that affect your budget significantly. Labor costs on the coasts for designers, technical specialists, programmers, and others tend to be double that in the middle of the continent. In 2000, programmers are making $85,000 a year straight out of college on the coasts.

Breaking Down the Budget

No matter what your budget level, you would want to allocate at least 10 percent for the analysis and planning phase. See Appendix A for a detailed project plan that shows exactly what is included in this phase. The remaining 90 percent of the budget would go to initial buildup. The majority of that cost would go to creating the interface, if you are starting from scratch. If you already have a site that you are reevaluating from a strategic perspective, the majority of the remaining budget would probably go toward technology and internal infrastructure.

Maintenance Budget

Last, but certainly not least, remember you are not building a thing but launching a service. It will need to be staffed, operated, evaluated, and improved. Don't forget to allocate an annual budget for maintenance and improvement of your Web site. This is not a one-time project.

Your maintenance activities will begin as soon as the site goes live. Costs for this activity will probably be in the same fiscal year as your initial start-up costs, so don't forget to budget for it immediately. For example, if it takes you three months to build your site, your maintenance activities would begin in the fourth month.

Typically, your annual maintenance budget should be about 33 percent of your initial outlay. So, if you are spending $50,000 on the initial buildup of Web activities, be sure to budget another $15,000 to $20,000 for maintenance and improvement activities.

Of course, this figure presumes that you already have a technology-training program in place for your employees. If you don't—and many companies still do not—be sure to add an additional amount for training.

Budgeting Time

The length of time needed to complete the initial build of a Web site varies greatly. Companies have been known to spend as little as one week or as much as one year or more to build a site. Even so, I've found that very little of strategic relevance gets done in less than three months. And if your company does not currently have a holistic business strategy—if your culture still perceives a Web site to be a separate part of the business—you will need three to six months just to bring about minimal culture change.

Summary

Of course, I can't build your site for you. No one knows your business like you. What I've attempted to do in this chapter is provide you with an approach to building your site that will assure that you incorporate those individuals who best know how to construct your site, whether they represent customer interests or technological know-how. Now, put names to some of the roles, spend some time with the project plan in Appendix A, and get your feet wet today.

8

GETTING TO REAL TIME

![Introduction marker] **Introduction**

How many times have you accessed a Web site with hopelessly outdated information? Does it make you want to do business with the company? Many companies put a great deal of funding and effort into creating a Web page but don't put the same emphasis on maintaining it. The Web is not a one-off project. It is an expansion of the business and should be treated as such. It is imperative that you have a plan of action for the routine operations of the Web site. Otherwise, your Web site will leave a negative impression of your company with your audience, customers and potential customers alike.

The basic questions that need to be answered about the operation of the site are:

- *What?* What are the information and functions in the site?
- *Who?* Who are the people responsible for keeping the project going?
- *How?* How do the technical and operational people plan for success?
- *When?* When should the site be developed, deployed, and maintained?

What?—Functional Content

Once you've set goals and selected an audience, it's time to start thinking about Web site content. Content consists of the words, images, and sounds used to create new ideas for interactive information services. Content provides the functionality that will attract your audience to your site. You know you're going to need to develop content, but you just don't know where to begin.

Most online media projects get bogged down with mining of the content. To many, the term *content* is synonymous with *words* or *pictures*. This conception leads to a focus on information rather than function. But information is only a part of the total content.

When I refer to content, it is synonymous with *function*. Not all information serves a function. Press releases are an excellent example of information that has no inherent function. If you feel that the information found in the press releases is of value to your audience, there is no harm in putting it on the Web site—if you also make it functional. For example, you may make press releases searchable so that your audience can quickly locate the information they need. You need to make your information do something.

Crutchfield.com is a long-time electronics catalog company. One of their best-selling categories is stereo equipment for automobiles. To put their catalog online, an enormous amount of information needs to be handled. Even equipping the site with a search engine isn't enough; the information is still too difficult for the customer to manage. Crutchfield's Web designers have designed a database system that will request the make, model, and year of the vehicle in which you wish to install the equipment. From then on, the catalog will show you only the equipment that will fit your car.

Better Than Paper

Your first temptation will be to dump everything you now have in print—books, brochures, articles—onto the site. Don't do it. You first need to analyze how the content works, how it is interrelated with other content in the service, and how the user interacts with the information. Often, this process results in a complete rework of the content—developing new work that is better suited to interactive technology but which achieves the original communications or learning objective.

Don't assume that just because something is in writing, it is worth putting online. Remember that information may be in writing because it is best suited to a paper format. For example, a very large detailed map will be very grainy and hard to read on a Web site.

Your Web site is not a book. It must be better than a book. It must be an interactive extension of your company. It must *improve* and *extend* your business communications process. It must provide a level of value and functionality that *no other medium* can provide. Toyota's Web site (www.toyota.com) is an excellent example. The site uses communications tools such as an interactive color picker that sell the cars better than a flat ad could.

There are many native benefits to online media. I highlight five of them here. Remember them in choosing content candidates.

Benefit 1: Online Media Is Dynamic, Timely, and Accurate. Online media is not static. Information flows and is constantly being updated to address the information needs of the individual. Online media can become the authoritative sources of information for a customer, vendor, or employee.

Some of the most dynamic Web sites are found in the financial markets. Companies such as E*Trade, Datek, and National Discount Brokers provide a live window into the markets, giving real-time market quotes and other data. Most of these companies even present a live "ticker" on the screen with continually updated stock quotes. This dynamic information is key to the growth of the online brokerage market. According to the Securities and Exchange Commission, in 1999 over 25 percent of all trades originated online!

Financial information is not the only kind of live data that can be put online. The electronics retailer J&R Music World, a large and successful New York company, offers shoppers live, real-time inventory status on its Web site.

Benefit 2: Online Media Is Responsive. The two-way nature of online media allows a service to proactively anticipate and deliver content that is formulated to meet the needs of the individual. The service is constantly in a feedback loop, monitoring and adapting the information presented. Although other companies did it first, Amazon.com set the standard for responsiveness via e-mail when it began sending order confirmations immediately after an order was placed and then sending shipping information as soon as the product left the warehouse. This level of responsiveness is now the standard expectation for companies doing business online.

Benefit 3: Online Media Is Searchable. Online media helps people discover new ways of finding information, formulating responses, and presenting information through the use of sophisticated searching of large information spaces. The ability to search is commonplace on the Internet, but the ability to *find* is less common. Many Web sites offer keyword searching, but some have moved beyond this basic functionality. One such site is Ask.com, which accepts natural language questions. For example, the question, "What is the weather in Tokyo?" will, as expected, bring up a weather report for Tokyo. This capability seems rather common sense; however, at the current state of the art, this is an advanced capability. Another interesting development in search technology can be found at Google.com. Rather than searching for words or phrases, this service bases search results on the number of pages linked to a given page. Thus, if 100 Web sites have links to information about geology, but seventy of them link to the same five sites, Google assumes that those five sites must be more "relevant." This technology works very well and is maturing rapidly.

Benefit 4: Online Media Is Protected. Protection of data is very important, so information is protected from exposure using a matrix of group and individual privileges. Sophisticated encryption tools are used to encrypt data. There have been no reported cases of encrypted data traveling over the Internet being decrypted while in transit. In fact, data-in-transit is quite well protected on the Internet. But once that data arrives at its destination, it is at risk for being compromised unless it is properly protected. Companies report having had credit card data stolen from their Web servers as a result of poor data management and poor network security policies.

Benefit 5: Online Media Is Accountable. One of the best features about doing business online is the built-in audit trail capabilities of the technology. Each time a Web site is accessed, a detailed record of the activities is recorded in a server log. This is a record of the date and time a page was seen, the length of time a page was viewed, and other technical information.

With the addition of "cookies," which are small blocks of text sent to and from your Web server and the user's computer, it is possible to track results more carefully.

The server sends a cookie file to the user's computer. Usually, the file includes a serial number of some kind and perhaps the date and time of the last time the user's computer connected to the Web site. Other information can be stored in a cookie file as well. As good example of this technique is how the online store Amazon.com greets customers by name when they "return" to the store. The Amazon.com server looks on the user's computer hard drive for the cookie file it placed there and then matches the customer serial number with a customer profile. The result is that Amazon.com has a unique customer profile it uses to make recommendations to its customers. The ultimate result of this approach is far more accountable media and marketing programs.

The most basic example of a tracking system in place is with banner advertisements. Most major

Web sites (such as Yahoo! and CNBC) have banner advertising included in their pages. These advertisements are "served" by a third-party advertising service. (Companies such as DoubleClick.net and 24/7 Media are major players in this space.)

Along with the advertisement itself, the third-party service sends a small text file (the "cookie") to your computer. This cookie file is the core of the "accountability" of the advertising medium. The cookie file is read by the ad server computers as you go from site to site, ensuring that you see advertising that is relevant to your interests. Unlike other advertising (such as newspapers or radio), with online advertising you know precisely how well your ads are working. You know what ads have been seen, what ads were "clicked" on, and what ads resulted in a sale.

Advertising is not the only area of accountability. Server activity records will quickly reveal what pages are getting the most views and what pages are being ignored. Reports on the page statistics can be generated by a wide range of programs (WebTrends™ at www.webtrends.com is very popular). The online magazine Salon.com uses these reporting tools daily to determine what pages and sections are the most popular with users. Writers at Salon.com, most of whom came from major newsmagazines and newspapers, were shocked at first to see how "ruthless" these reports were; they had a hard time accepting that their articles were not read by as many people as they first thought would be reading them.

Adapting Existing Content

Although you need to be very careful not to merely dump existing documents onto the Web site, you would be a fool not to analyze current material for its appropriateness. Many software products are starting to offer "hooks" into Web publishing. For example, the contact management program Now Up To Date offers a simple Web server system to let others view the master calendar through a Web browser.

Below are four examples of where you might find content for your Web site in your current organization, and what it might take to adapt it.

Source 1: Databases. There is no reason you cannot make databases available on the Internet. Virtually any major database system can be accessed through a Web browser interface such as Microsoft Access, Oracle, Sybase, and FileMaker. You can even get software to link other databases, such as mainframes or legacy systems (current offerings include WebObjects and ColdFusion).

For example, the financial software company

Hyperion has direct links into a Lotus Notes database of trade events through its Web pages. One person inside Hyperion maintains the company's database of events, and the entire world gains access to this information.

Another company that managed to turn database information into useful "content" is American Express. Through the company's Web site (www.americanexpress.com), you can see all your transactions, pay your bill, even download information into popular financial management software such Quicken™.[1] The data is updated in real time. The same information that is available to the phone service representatives is available to you.

Source 2: Printed Materials. Electronic source files, when they exist, can speed up the process of adapting print media to online media. All current versions of document production software offer some level of direct HTML output: Microsoft Word, Excel, Lotus WordPro, and WordPerfect.

The annual report is quite possibly one of the most boring documents in history, but Microsoft has been a leader in making its annual reports into useful analytical tools. By using online communications, the company facilitates the creation of meaningful information from the raw data encompassed in its annual reports. Most other companies do not do this.

IKEA, the Swedish company that sells home furnishings worldwide, has also done some interesting experiments turning print materials into online content. It does so with a product called Shockwave, which is a program used to create simple, cartoonlike animations. (For an extensive gallery of Shockwave animations, see www.shockwave.com.) These animations are used to bring assembly instruction manuals to life. Although the company has created only a few animations showing how to put together bookshelves, the possibilities are intriguing.

Another company that uses Shockwave to convert printed materials to animated instructional services is Netday (Web site: www.netday.org). Netday is a nationwide organization dedicated to wiring schools for Internet access. On its Web site are instructional pieces that show how to connect the wiring for network connection jacks. These simple instructions allow community members with no experience in wiring networks to quickly learn how to use the wiring tools correctly.

Source 3: Multimedia. Be careful in adapting multimedia such as video and audio; it is very bandwidth hungry and should be used only when it is clearly needed. One of the more interesting multimedia adaptations available is "streaming" media (sometimes called *net casting*), which is audio or video sent out over the Internet in real time. Company meetings, investor earnings reports, and other "content" can be adapted and put into use via the Internet through use of this technology. Companies such as 3M, Intel, Yahoo!, and Cisco all use streaming media for critical events such as analyst meetings and shareholder meetings. But it does not take the financial resources of huge companies such as these to put a streaming media event together. In fact, using the free Microsoft product NetMeeting, even a small business can do a basic net cast of a PowerPoint™ slide show.

Source 4: Purchased Dynamic Content. Live content can be very interesting parts of your site. Live content may include news feeds, stocks, weather, or alerting systems. Table 8.1 lists various suppliers of live content. Be sure that the type of content you choose fills a need for your target consumer.

Streaming media is often available for purchase. You can put just about any useful information on your site. Some services will build a specific filter for your site so that you can have newswires and other updates on your site that are most pertinent to your audience. They can

Table 8.1 Types of Dynamic Content.

General News Feeds	Many offerings including CNN (www.cnn.com) & ABC News (www.abcnews.com)
Tailored News Feeds	Individual Inc. (www.individual.com) & Reuters (www.reuters.com).
Stock Tickers	Bigcharts.com & Reuters (www.reuters.com)
Weather Maps	Freese-Notis Weather (www.weather.net) & The Weather Channel™ (www.weather.com)
Alerting Systems	Information via e-mail (www.mercury.com); or the Microsoft Internet Explorer™ "Channels" concept (www.cnn.com); or Netscape Netcaster™ functionality.

include such media as weather forecasts, sports, *Red Herring Magazine, Salon, Christian Science Monitor*, and so on.

Creating New Content

You can always create fresh content for your Internet business, but it can be extremely time consuming to create content that is of value to your audience.

Many companies propose posting daily news and other "soft" information to encourage use of the system. Unfortunately, soft content, although easy to develop, is not as valuable as "hard" content (for example, production reports, facts and figures, and job assignments). The value of these hard-content items is higher to the user and will create higher use patterns.

You would be much better off to maximize your ability to publish hard content through group publishing techniques (discussed later in this chapter).

A Word of Caution

You might think you own a piece of content, but it's easy to be fooled. For example, most publicly traded companies outsource the publication of their annual report. There are many cases in which that annual report is licensed only for print and only to be distributed to shareholders. Although the corporation might think they own the information found in the annual report, they might not have the rights to reproduce that report online or on CD-ROM. Be especially careful to obtain electronic reproduction rights for every piece you wish to put on the Internet.

Even new work should be created under a work-for-hire agreement so as to avoid future legal battles. Double-check contracts with all free-lancers or contractors of any kind (including those writing your computer code).

Also, several companies are writing into their employment agreements releases for use of employees' photographs. If there is no release, you might be liable for damages if you use the employees' pictures. In New York, companies are beginning to write up releases for employees' pictures for the dual purpose of using them in security badges and in promotional materials.

Finally, as you are content mining, you might find an item for which you need permission from someone who is unaware of the need. Sometimes going to that person for permission opens up a bigger can of worms than simply redoing the piece. If the content is fairly simple, you might want to re-create it in-house.

These cautionary tales are merely examples. I advise you to have a lawyer review your content before it is completed. If there is any doubt about the ownership of your content, it must be checked thoroughly to ensure that clear rights are obtained to reproduce the content.

Who?—The Role of the Traditional Web Master

Chapter 7 already went into a great deal of detail about how to structure the initial set-up of the Web site and major modifications to the site. But as part of your day-to-day business, you will need to set up an operations procedure.

Most companies have established the role of "Web master" as a central point of responsibility for the actual operation of the site. In general, this person, or occasionally group of people, takes all of the content items and adapts them for the Web as needed.

Advantages of the Traditional Web Master Approach

There are several advantages to the traditional Web master–as–interface approach.

First, it establishes a single point of responsibility for online communications. This set-up makes it easier to focus and direct efforts because only one person or group will be responsible for the Web site.

Second, Web masters typically have the tools and resources to adapt almost any content to an online presentation. This capability makes it easier for the people to "feed" content to the Web master.

Third, because the Web master is often the one who developed the Web site originally, she or he is more likely to have a zeal for the Web site that other employees may not have. This grass-roots zeal for Web development is even stronger in intranet projects. Furthermore, many times Web projects are "fringe" projects, and other employees simply don't have the interest or resources it would take to maintain the Web site.

Disadvantages of the Traditional Web Master Approach

The solo Web master served many companies well in the first four or five years of the Internet revolution. These "grass-roots" efforts continue. However, beleaguered Web masters typically find themselves overwhelmed by far too much work with far too little resources and no strategic direction.

The Web master is not always able to maintain a timely Web site. This outcome is especially likely as the project requirements grow and the Web master finds himself or herself responsible for vast quantities of content.

The Web master has final control of all online content but rarely has the necessary strategic direction to accomplish his or her goal. Despite outward appearances of the company having control over the content and design, ultimately the Web master controls the look and feel of the site. There have been instances of companies that have had Web masters refuse to build content for the site because they "didn't like it."

The Web master is a Web guru, but this person isn't always able to maintain a strategic focus. The now-famous IBM "Flaming Logo" commercial has a Web master showing a manager the company logo with animated flames on it. The manager asks the Web master, "Why is our logo flaming?" To which the Web master replies, "Because it's on fire." It's funny not only because of the delivery of lines by the actors but also because it's painfully true for many companies. Too often, the Web master loses focus on the strategic aspects of the Internet or intranet project in favor of providing technically interesting content.

It is fairly easy to spot a Web site with a Web master. It will have little or no "real" information, links to live back-end systems, and often visual interfaces that are inconsistent. This is not for lack of effort or trying on the part of the Web master; it is because a nearly solo effort simply can't provide and maintain an enterprisewide communications system.

Specifically, having a single Web master also means having a single point of failure. One person has responsibility for the entire interactive presentation of the company.

The Web Master as Facilitator

The Web master role has changed from a content focus to a process focus. It has become that of communications ombudsman, who can integrate the systems, develop the operations, and monitor the overall health of the Web site. The Web master role has evolved into the e-business manager of the interactive council.

The person performing this job now:

- Builds the technical infrastructure
- Develops templates for a consistent "look and feel" to Web pages
- Enables group publishing structures
- Creates e-commerce standards and solutions
- Handles the information movement infrastructure

The Web master is not a content developer, a designer, or a programmer. She becomes the point of contact for integration of infostructures.

Don't dissolve your interactive council once the Web page is initially off the ground. Council members should continue to meet on at least a quarterly basis to coordinate improvements to the Web site and the strategic direction of the e-business. For example, if you decide to move toward a wireless strategy, you will still need a council to manage the development of that strategy. The interactive council becomes a strategic planning entity as the business moves to real time.

How?—The Group Publishing Model

Group publishing is the natural extension of the new role of the Web master. It also ties in quite nicely with the corporate infostructure discussed in Chapter 6. With group publishing, the Web master builds systems that let the company update the site itself as a result of its regular workflow. Wherever possible, sources should have hypertext markup language (HTML) publishing capabilities to directly publish to the Web site without intervention by a Web master (see Figure 8.1). Of course, giving users direct publishing capabilities means that the Web master must have a great deal of political as well as technical skill. It also means that an infostructure must be firmly in place so that employees understand what their responsibilities are.

Figure 8.1 Group Publishing.

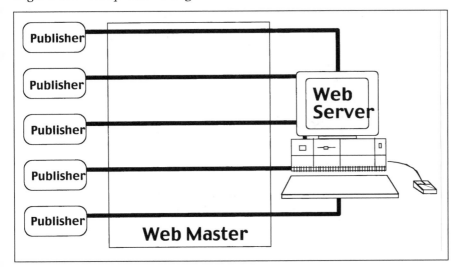

Virtually every news site on the Internet uses some form of group publishing. One of the earliest companies to really leverage group publishing effectively was CINet, a technology news service (www.cnet.com and www.news.com). So successful was their implementation that they created a software product—StoryServer, marketed by Vignette—that allows multiple authors to compose parts of a Web site concurrently. It is used by news organizations such as CNN to allow reporters to submit their stories directly to the main Web site with no Web master intervention.

News sites are not the only beneficiaries of group publishing. Ford uses group publishing to keep technical manuals up to date. The U.S. Navy uses a publishing system called eGroups (www.egroups.com) to coordinate some shipbuilding projects. Group publishing really is what the Net is all about.

Advantages of Group Publishing

Of course, there are numerous advantages to a group publishing approach. First, it is much faster than publishing individually, and one's Web site is more likely to be up-to-date. As information changes, those responsible for the information can update the Web site. There is no need to stop for the Web master.

Second, group publishing is more accurate than publishing individually online. By eliminating the conversion step, the possibility of making errors is decreased. Finally, this approach is more authoritative, because the information comes directly from the source.

Disadvantages of Group Publishing

Of course, some would point out that the advantages can also be disadvantages. The group publishing approach can be too fast. There is no checkpoint, so it is a lot easier for *misinformation* to be published as well.

Second, group publishing entails inherent higher training costs. Employees will have to have a greater understanding of their computers and of the Internet.

Third, cultural differences can be a big factor. Many people are uncomfortable with the absence of a buffer between the publisher and the public.

When?—Keeping the Web Site Up to Date

On the Web there needs to be a dynamic signaling of "newness" to retain the user's attention. This goal is accomplished by keeping the site very current.

When organizing to keep your site up to date, it is important to be realistic about how frequently information changes. Some items, such as mission statements or office locations, are "evergreen" and not subject to frequent change. But most information items should have an expiration date. Develop a "latency table" that indicates who is responsible for the information and when it is to be reviewed and updated. Figure 8.2 is an example of a latency table. Notice that not only does it assign frequency of updates to all content areas but it also assigns responsibility and a backup for that update. This step is critical. Group publishing does not work without a clear definition of how the work will get done.

Of course, Web updates should always be timed to correspond with changes in information. Coordinate update schedules with overall marketing and business plans to keep the site in line with current marketing activities. Figure 8.3 shows a sample calendar. Notice that the updates are scheduled to occur after review meetings or right before a new product launch. The Web is

Figure 8.2 Latency Table.

Content Item	Info. Authority	Backup	Updates
Price Sheet	MF	BW	Weekly
Open Orders	JH	KW	Continually
Mission Statement	DG	SK	Evergreen

Figure 8.3 Update Schedules.

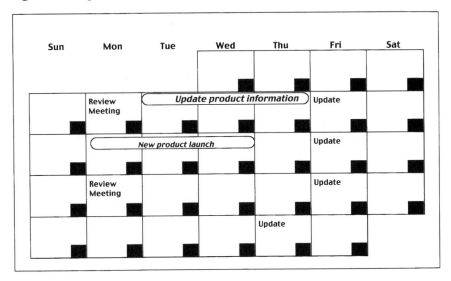

an extension of your business, and Web activities should be timed to coincide with corollary business activities.

Summary

It helps to have all these systems in place before the Web site is operational. If not, you risk creating a negative image of your company in the electronic space. But if you haven't already formed an operational plan, now is the time to do it. You will be able to provide value to your audience through functional content and timely information, and with group publishing you will be able to do it much more efficiently than you ever have. Maintenance of the Web site should not be an expensive or disruptive proposition. Rather, this task should be integrated into everyday business activities just like any other part of your business. After all, your online presence may be the only interface you have with some customers.

9

ESTABLISHING RETURN ON INVESTMENT

Introduction

At this point, you might have ongoing e-commerce. You have established project goals, and you are measuring them. But how do you convince upper management of the success of your project when they aren't particularly interested in the technology? Return on investment (ROI) is one of the most popular measures of any project success, electronic or otherwise. There is no reason this measure can't be applied to Internet business ventures. You invest in your Web site, and you either generate cost savings or income/value. You wouldn't do otherwise.

There are three basic approaches to finding the ROI on your Internet venture: cost chain analysis, value chain analysis, and transaction chain analysis. Each of these techniques is best suited to value generated in one of three different "zones." Each technique overlaps the other slightly. However, together they form a conceptual basis for simple ROI analysis of the site.

Zone 1: Real-Time Information

Zone 1 encompasses those pieces of information that are not interactive but need to be moved to various audiences. Typically, the Internet replaces fax and paper distribution for these pieces of information, which are common and easy to develop. Many times this type of information is static, consisting of, for example, policies and procedures, store locations, or directions to the office. Many items that are not static, however, would also qualify for zone 1. Such items are currently distributed as static items and involve no interaction. A company phone list would be a perfect example of information that changes frequently but which is often treated as a static list. This frequently updated information often has the highest return on investment. In this case, there is also an opportunity for an even higher return by creating an active database on the Web site rather than leaving it as a list.

Cost Chain Analysis

Cost chains are the easiest to construct of all the ROI calculators. They are both simple and effective in establishing hard cost savings measurements and are usually used as a way of measuring the cost/benefit of moving information that is currently in paper form. Use cost chains where specific manual processes can be replaced with automated ones.

For example, it is clear that the cost of printing and faxing a document is higher than distributing the same information online. A cost chain analysis of the process of sending a fax can generate some remarkable results.

Figure 9.1 shows a sample cost chain analysis for printing and faxing information. Assume that an administrative assistant is sending routine information to a potential customer. In this case, the total cost of faxing this information is $5.29. To determine cost savings, you would need to mul-

Figure 9.1 Sample Cost Chain: Faxing Information.

Action	Task	Labor (Minutes)	Labor Hourly Rate	Materials	Cost for Materials	Timed or Per Use Services	Timed Per Use Units	Cost of Timed Per Use	Total
Incoming Call WATS	Talk on Phone	5.00	$14.00			WATS Line	5.00	$0.14	$1.87
Send a Product Brochure by Fax	Find Brochures	3.00	14.00						$0.70
	Printouts	3.00	14.00	2 Laser Printed Sheets	$0.10				$0.80
	Baby-sit Fax	5.00	14.00			Fax Toll Call	5.00	0.15	$1.92
								Grand Total	$5.29

tiply the number of downloads of the same information (a basic server statistic) by $5.29.

Now, the number of downloads of a particular document have more than just statistical interest—they have bottom-line impact. These cost savings can be applied to your ROI formula.

Zone 2: Transactions, Commerce, and Tools

A transaction is not simply buying something online. A transaction or tool, for the purposes of this discussion, is any exchange of information that sets into motion action or activity external to the online service and results in a tangible benefit to the end user. While many transactions are revenue generating, others are not. For example, completing a time sheet is a transaction, as is updating a customer record. In zone 2, information:

- Changes frequently
- Requires real-time transport
- Is often linked to legacy systems (see Chapter 7)
- Is interactive

These items have their ROI measured best by a string of cost chains, which make up a *transaction chain.*

Transaction Chain Analysis

A transaction chain is nothing more than a string of cost chains associated with a series of actions needed to complete a larger task. The important variable in a transaction chain is that the cost chains are started by something an end user does, not what the Web master decides the site will do. Thus, a person ordering parts through the Web site causes a series of small cost chains to interact.

To begin constructing a transaction chain, you need to identify the path that information takes from the start of a transaction to its conclusion. Figure 9.2 illustrates a transaction chain with which we are all familiar: ordering a pizza. The *initiating action* is the action that starts the transaction. In this case, it would be either a

Figure 9.2 Pizza Ordering Transaction Chain.

Step	Methods and Systems Used
Initiating Action	Telephone
Data Collection	Ears, Pencils
Data Recording	Notepad, Cash Register
Data Distribution	Ticket on Order Rack
Action Taken	Make Pizza, Send It to Buyer

phone call or store visit. *Data collection* follows the initiating action. In this case, it might be a handwritten form. In other cases it might be touch-tone key hits or direct entry to a terminal system. *Data recording* might be the same action as data collection or it might be a separate step. Is the data rekeyed into another data collection system? Or is the paper form the one means of data recording? *Data distribution* is the next step. How does the person who takes your order tell the cook how to make it or the delivery person where to go? The message could be sent by voice, computer system, fax, or other means. Finally an *action* is taken. The pizza is made and delivered. Of course, the customers only see the end result—they get the pizza. They don't care how the transaction chain works.

Figure 9.3 shows a more sophisticated example of a transaction chain. This time you can see how an online ordering process might be completed.

Figure 9.3 Transaction Chain: Online Ordering Process.

Step	Methods and Systems Used
Initiating Action	User accesses order form from the online service. User fills out the form and submits it for processing.
Data Collection	Web server parses data from HTML form and sends it to back-end database.
Data Recording	Oracle database reads in data from Web, creates new transaction record and performs necessary data processing to generate pick ticket, authorize credit card, and update daily sales reports.
Data Distribution	Pick ticket is issued to warehouse floor, shipping information passed to shipping area.
Action Taken	New pick ticket causes worker to get item from shelf packed and shipped for customer. Data about transaction recorded in master database.

For each transaction you intend to offer on your Web site, you would want to construct a transaction chain. Some transactions you might consider would be product literature requests, customer technical support questions, purchases of goods, reservations for an event, and so on.

Analyzing transaction chains has a side benefit. Because transaction chain analysis looks at the overall workflow process and methods, it can be used to identify cost savings where electronic activities may streamline the transaction. Remember, the more you can combine activities, shortening the transaction chain, the more cost savings you will incur.

Let's take the example of the distribution of a document that must be mailed out for legal or customer preference reasons. To create the trans-

Figure 9.4 Example Transaction: Collateral Material Mailing.

Current Steps	Proposed
1. Incall at call center	1. Customer selects materials
2. Qualify request	desired from Web page
3. Key-in customer information	2. Customer enters shipping info
4. Print request information	3. Shipping request prints in
5. Fax to collateral distribution	collateral distribution center
6. Consolidate materials requests	4. Pull materials
7. Pull materials	5. Pack
8. Pack	6. Mail
9. Mail	
Processing Cost: $14.80	Processing Cost: $6.72

action chain, identify the steps involved and
assign a cost to each of those steps by using a
series of cost chain analysis tables. Figure 9.4
shows what this transaction chain might look
like. The first column presents the current state
transaction chain. But notice the second column, which highlights cost savings for an electronic process. The difference between the two
processes can be an input to the ROI formula.

As you can see, transaction analysis is a far more
powerful process than simply identifying cost
savings. It identifies possibilities for Web site
workflow integration—ways that an online communications system would address and compress
the transaction and improve it for the customer.

The transaction chain looks at information flow
into and out of a company and seeks to automate

where appropriate and streamline where possible. This is why transaction analysis can be very helpful in Web development stages. The transaction chain is less concerned with the cost of moving the information (which is assessed in a cost chain) than it is with the process of causing information to be moved or an action to be taken within the company.

Zone 3: Relationship and Value Exchange

In zone 3, you are measuring the value of the site. You're not simply looking at ways of cutting costs while continuing in the same activities you've always done. You're looking at new value added by the site itself.

In this zone, you will find that your activities don't seem to have a clear bottom-line impact in the same way that zones 1 and 2 do, but this is a misconception. You have to consider the *value* to the organization of your online activities. For example, what is the value of a fully qualified lead? By *fully qualified* I mean a lead coming into the sales organization where all of the contact information is known, the needs of the lead have been assessed, and possibly a product or service line has been selected for further exploration. This effort requires the measurement of the value of the prequalified lead.

The value often ties very closely to marketing efforts. You may be looking at Internet-only promotional offers, banner advertising, co-marketing agreements, sponsorships, personalized or targeted content pages, and the like.

Value Chain Analysis

Value chains ultimately are a measure of the success of the various calls to action and the continued value of the Web site to the customer. The value chain analysis measures the way in which the site achieves less tangible value, such as "improved response to customer requests" and "more effective lead qualification." The value analyzed here is much more difficult to put a hard number on, but you'll find that in many cases simple business analysis will allow you to put some reasonable figures here.

A typical example of a value chain is the cost of customer acquisition. There are many ways of acquiring a customer—for example, by advertising or direct mail. These activities all involve costs. All of these costs are incurred as part of establishing the brand, presenting the value proposition, and providing a call to action to go to the next step and become a customer. In this case, you might look to the number of new customers generated from your site: 100,000 unique visitors over 30 days resulted in 1,000 new customers. You could then apply this to the ROI formula as income generated.

A trickier example of a value chain is customer retention. You might know that 73 percent of the users of the Web site are repeat visitors who use the site daily or that of the 1,000 customers acquired in January, 985 were still customers in December. These figures give you some idea of overall customer retention. You will need to take these statistics to the next level, though, to apply them to the ROI formula. How does the retention of Web customers compare to that of traditional customers? You could clearly put a dollar value on a high retention rate. But this effort would ignore overall business customer retention rates. You might have to go to customer surveys to get a clearer picture of these retention rates. For example, if your traditional customers were converting to Web customers, the difference in the retention of customers using traditional channels and those using online channels might be quite high. Online customers might be much more loyal than traditional customers, for example, or they might be much less loyal. But even without an increase in customer retention for the company there might be a significant benefit.

A good cautionary tale comes from Merrill Lynch, which used to say that online investing was "bad for America," when in fact it was just bad for their existing business model. After publicly stating many times that Merrill Lynch would "never" get into online trading, the company reversed field in the summer of 1999 and launched a primitive and expensive online trading system. Although Merrill Lynch is not in any imminent danger of failing as an ongoing firm, in the spring of 2000, the company laid off 12 percent of its staff, a cost-cutting move to make it more competitive in a changed marketplace. You might be avoiding a significant drop in customer retention by establishing Web options. This uncertainty is what makes value chain analysis so difficult. You might also want to look at brand awareness, customer satisfaction, impact of advertising, and other factors.

The impact of Internet advertising on a car dealership provides an illustration. Let's say it costs a large car dealer $1,200 in traditional advertising and promotions to get a person to come to the showroom and take a test drive of a new car. The dealer spends $112,000 a month on traditional media, and this expenditure generates ninety to ninety-five leads. If the dealer can measure how many leads result from its Internet activities, it can generate a similar cost-per-lead figure. In this case, the car dealer allows potential customers to sign up online for a test drive appointment, so the dealer is able to determine that thirty people a month come directly from the Internet site. If the initial cost of the site were $8,000, those leads would cost $267 per lead—a savings of over $900 a month. But let's say the site generates forty leads the next month. Since the site's already established, it costs only $1,500 to maintain. Now the leads only cost $37.50 to generate.

Of course, this situation isn't as simple as it looks. You can continue digging through the data. You might want to analyze how qualified these new leads are: Are you selling to them at the same rate? a better rate?

Remember, value chains analyze the value created through your Web site. How well does your site generate leads, provide a call to action, support the customer, or build the brand? You must figure out a way to quantify the value if you want it to be part of your ROI formula. Here are some simple tricks to help you measure the value that your Web site generates.

- Provide a unique 1-800 number on the Web site, then track which sales came from that number.
- Develop a Web-only offer and track the number of responses to the offer.
- Offer a discount for purchases made on the Web and track increases in sales on the Web.

ROI Case Studies

Of course, most Web sites encompass activities in all three zones. You cannot get a solid ROI measurement without looking at all three in combination. To give you a better feel for how to approach this, I've included two case studies here.

Dell Computer

Dell Computer had specialized in direct build-to-order sales for a long time before moving to the Web. They essentially moved to the Web because it was ideally suited to their business model. They were able to easily leverage their existing infrastructure and systems. In 2000, Dell computer was selling over $23 million a day in computer hardware over the Internet.[1]

Zone 1. Because of Dell's business model (they build hardware when it is ordered, thus minimizing inventory), their product information is changing rapidly. In fact, because they turn inventory thirty-two times per year, their product offerings need to be updated continuously. The online service dramatically reduces costs for distributing this information.

Zone 2. Dell is able to significantly shorten transaction chains for hardware purchases through the Web site. Information from Dell's interactive pricing screens is fed directly into the company's order processing and factory assembly system. The computer is built, credit cards are charged, and the accounting system is updated.

Zone 3. Dell is able to provide extra value to the customer through a highly dynamic interactive price calculator that allows potential customers to generate a quote immediately without having to call in. The customer can play "what-if?" with their configuration, adding and removing components and getting a price on the spot. If a customer wants to buy the system as defined by the interactive tool, he need only click a "Buy it" button, and the transaction processor is activated. Even if the customer chooses to call the company 1-800 number, he is given the advantage of having specified exactly which system he intends to buy, saving time for the customer and Dell.

Amazon.com

Amazon.com is a relatively new company that came into being as a result of Internet technologies. The company provides an extremely strong business model for online retailing based on principles of marketing and brokering sales. Although Amazon.com is still best known for its book division, the company now applies this business model to other retailing sectors. It keeps very little physical inventory. Instead, it brokers sales through other distributors.

Zone 1. Amazon.com has an extensive catalog of available merchandise that is continually updated. It minimizes costs by distributing this information only over the Internet. The information is never printed, and the company does not take phone orders.

Zone 2. Amazon.com has minimized costs by shortening the online ordering transaction to almost nothing. Its order processing system is the standard by which others are judged. With its "one-click" ordering, the company literally reduces the entire buying process to clicking an icon.

Zone 3. Amazon.com is able to add value to the customer experience with a variety of custom services and tools. Most notably, its recommendation service makes intelligent associations based on a customer's past purchases and similar books in a genre.

Summary

The ROI generated in each of these three zones can be totaled to determine an overall project ROI. Although calculating total ROI for electronic commerce might not be simple, it certainly is the most accepted measure of project success. You will probably find that your Web project is given higher consideration if you can establish an ROI that meets company objectives. But don't forget to point out that ROI is not the only measure of success. Some benefits, such as an improvement in customer loyalty, might be particularly difficult to quantify. Don't get hung up on the calculation of the numbers. In the case of e-commerce, certain minimum expectations must be met simply to stay in business, even if they appear to have high up-front costs.

10

IT'S
TIME
TO ACT

"The future is where we're all going to live, so we might as well get with the program now."

—Neal Stephenson,
author of *Snow Crash* and *The Diamond Age*
and co-author of *The Difference Engine*

■■■■ Introduction

There is no time like the present to start your e-business. You simply cannot delay any longer. It would be foolhardy to say e-business is not relevant to your industry. Even if you happen to be in an industry that lags behind on technology, it will be here before you know it.

Some day very soon, the "e" in e-business will evaporate. Electronic business will simply be business. In 1996 nobody had e-mail addresses on business cards. The e-commerce explosion came along in four short years. Why wouldn't the Web site become part of your overall infrastructure within the next four?

We now have an entire generation moving into the job market who grew up on the Net. They are now making important buying decisions. The purchasing agent at the local plant may be one of them. She just finished engineering school, where she signed up for classes, submitted homework, took final exams, sent letters, and made plans with friends, all online. Now her job is to specify and purchase materials, and she is more comfortable going online to order than schmoozing with a sales guy over lunch or leafing through catalogs. She wants complete information, total access, and instant gratification. You must be able to give it to her.

Of course, you not only need to be able to sell to this generation, you need to be able to hire and retain them. You need to be able to keep them interested, and this will be difficult without technology. Even in an economic downturn, the best talent will still go to companies that take complex processes and make them interesting.

Today, this generation is on the frontline of corporations. As they move up the corporate ladder and change roles, they will begin to set rules—rules for you, your clients, and your vendors. Are you ready?

Step by Step

If you don't have a Web site or if your Web site is still about the company and doesn't do something meaningful (that forces someone outside marketing to do work), you are not ready. It's time to start doing business. Your company is not going to change overnight, but there are things you can tackle right away.

Leaf through this book one more time. Look at who you are and who you want to be using the wild kingdom model in Chapter 2 and the planning model in Chapter 3. If you like what you see, you can launch right into a strategic e-business plan. Unfortunately, most of us don't like what we see.

If your company is truly not strategically positioned correctly, you will need to make some internal changes that may take six to nine months. You might start with cultural and technological change (Chapter 5) and infostructuring (Chapter 6).

But, at the same time, you could make some improvements to your company that bring you up to today's minimum expectations—immediately. Incidentally, making these changes will often help push your cultural changes along as well.

Pick two or three projects you can do now. They should be of real significance to your business. One place many chose to start is in the recruiting arm of the human resources department. It's not too difficult to post openings online, and all the recent college graduates are looking there (yes, even the liberal arts majors). Use posting boards like Monster.com, HotJobs.com, or Dice.com.

On the infrastructure side, you can always start moving your company toward more sophisticated technology solutions, even if you don't have a full understanding of how you will eventually use them strategically. For example, you might discover you need a customer database. You may have one use in mind now and find in six months you have another use for it. It doesn't matter that you weren't able to predict all possible uses; you still needed the database. You can start these projects with the confidence that they will still be relevant.

On the inside, you can often drive the decision to do back-office processes online. Force your purchasing agents to grow up and do their procurement online. In my practice, my clients all agree to accept electronic invoicing. Some of them aren't accustomed to doing it this way, but they all make it work on their end somehow— even the big companies. It saves me a fortune over paper billing. Of course, it would be even better to give clients the capability to pay their bills online with electronic bank transfers, so now I accept PayPal, an easy electronic payment system.

Don't start your e-business with the mass consumer market. That market can be quite fickle. Unless you are a retailer, a good interactive strategy generally ignores the public at large. Denise Caruso of the *New York Times* believes business-to-business commerce actually should have developed before retail applications of the Net— it just makes so much more sense.[1] Choose a couple of strategic vendors or clients and start online transactions. The transactions could be billing, issuing purchase orders, configuring products, closing sales deals, or exchanging money. When you have a good arrangement with a top business partner, the work you did for them can typically be replicated for others without much effort.

Remember, the change doesn't need to be systemic. The furniture industry tends to be a laggard when it comes to technology. Yet Steelcase is now offering an online quote generator and prequalifying sales online. They aren't actually closing the deal online today, but they've laid the groundwork.

Don't make the excuse that e-business is not a requirement in your industry. It will be soon. It doesn't matter if only two people a day are doing business with you online today. This gives you a unique chance to practice your next business model before it's a sink-or-swim situation. Take the opportunity to get a jump-start on your competition.

Finishing the Project

By this point you should know that designing your Web site is a project you will never truly finish. You will always be modifying and improving your site. At the same time, many companies find it difficult to let go of the project and actually put their page out on the Internet. Your Web site will never be perfect—so accept that fact and get on with your business.

The entire Internet is based on the theory that technology is "good enough." The "guts" of the Internet are themselves faulty at times. The protocols to transfer data don't always work. If the best you can do today is a template-driven out-of-the-box Web page, then do it just to have something up. Precision to the exclusion of action is nonsensical and detrimental to e-business. Just keep adjusting, improving, and refining.

Although the entire site may never be perfect, there may be parts of the site that have to be. For example, credit card processing must be exact. But product pictures probably shouldn't be; if they're too good, it will take too long to load them. Analyze which parts of your site have to be perfect and which parts just have to be there.

Of course, you don't want a sloppy site. Don't do ten things poorly if you can do two things well. Do the two things well first, and then you can gradually build in the other eight functions. Praxair, a supplier of gases, has built a nice informational site. It has no commerce, but it's a nice brochure. You, too, can make a nice informational site quickly. Then, like Praxair, you can add commerce functions a few at a time.

Federal Express also took things slowly. They started out with a public information site. Then they realized that the most important function for them strategically was to have the customer input his own transactions, using the same screens the company's customer service representatives were using. Linking customers to the customer service system through the Web site saved the courier service $4 million annually in telecommunications costs.[2] Federal Express gradually scaled their site up until the customer could do many tasks, such as preparing weigh bills, monitoring his own account, and scheduling pickups. The company built their site incrementally, picking strategically important functions first.

Summary

Look at how quickly the Internet has been accepted as a legitimate way of doing business. Interest builds from being mildly intriguing to being vitally important very quickly. The electronic economy has quickly moved from industry to industry.

No matter what stage your industry is currently in, it is time for you to start your e-commerce activities. If you wait until your traditional competitors are doing it, you will miss your opportunity and will find yourself constantly playing catch-up.

This is not merely a theory. It has been born out time and again by companies that did not recognize the value of the Internet until their competitors passed them by. Put yourself in the position of Merrill Lynch, which publicly stated that online trading was bad for the economy. The company was made a laughingstock and suffered permanent brand damage. People still view Merrill Lynch as a second-class online citizen. DLJ*direct*, on the other hand, was an old brokerage house that used the Internet as another channel to extend its business as a whole. The company was able to slip past Merrill Lynch.

I believe a number of well-known, formidable companies will be gone within five years because they didn't get their act together online. Startups are able to slip past the giants more easily than we would ever imagine. When was the last time you bought online? Have you bought from Amazon.com? (Most people would answer yes.) Have you bought from Kmart.com or any other mass retailer? (Most would say no.) The idea of online business has been exploited by the startups. Big insurance companies didn't use electronic commerce until Healtheon started streamlining medical information: patient records, medical records, doctor information, and so on. Much of the banking industry chose to ignore the Internet; now it is absolutely critical to credit card companies and mortgage brokers. There are reports that 70 percent of all mortgages are now researched online. The Internet-ready corporation, no matter how new or how small, will displace the giants that are not technologically ready.

Are you one of those giants? Or are you a smaller company that has chosen to ignore the Internet? You are in a precarious position. Your vendors and clients who are bigger than you may be in a position to force you to do business electronically just as the big three auto makers are doing to their vendors. Will you be forced out of business by your unpreparedness?

You are in a race, whether you like it or not. The time to act is now.

Ready, Set, GO!

Appendix A

THE WEB SITE DEVELOPMENT PROJECT PLAN

■ Analysis and Review Phase

Activity	Tasks	Deliverables
Business objectives review	❏ Meet with necessary staff to finalize the business objectives for the project	❏ Approved business objectives statement and project mission
Content planning	❏ Identify the specific existing content items to be incorporated into the site ❏ Obtain electronic versions of all existing content ❏ Identify the people and process needed to keep *existing* content current ❏ Identify new content to be created for the site ❏ Identify people and process needed to keep *new* content current	❏ Content list ❏ Site outline ❏ Site map ❏ Roles and responsibilities report
Technologies planning	❏ Identify the specific technologies needed for information publishing (Acrobat, NetObjects, HTML forms, server-side programming) ❏ Develop server specification	❏ Technical specifications and requirements document
Prototype development	❏ Develop three different "look and feel" explorations ❏ Present to project team ❏ Select look and feel for development ❏ Refine selected look and feel ❏ Create project timetable ❏ Create development budget	❏ Three look-and-feel designs, each with two example interfaces ❏ Final interface design specification ❏ Development budget and timetable

▬▬ Production Phase

Activity	Tasks	Deliverables
Initial development	❑ Convert legacy documents to HTML and PDF formats ❑ Develop HTML framework for site ❑ Integrate content and graphical layouts ❑ Construct all user interface pages ❑ Construct administrative interface pages	❑ Completed user interface ❑ Completed administrator interfaces (where appropriate)
Technical development	❑ Set up Web server hardware ❑ Set up Web server software ❑ Set up server logging software (if called for in the technical specifications) ❑ Develop administrative scripts and programs ❑ Load testing and evaluation of scripts and programs	❑ Configured Web server system ❑ Administrative software for content maintenance ❑ Configured software for site measurement (if measurement software is used)
Content integration and testing	❑ Integrate server-side software with user interface ❑ Integrate server-side software with administrative interface modules ❑ Conduct alpha testing ❑ Do a friendly beta test ❑ Publicly beta-test	❑ Server system loaded with appropriate initial content ❑ Coordinated bug reports ❑ Bug fixes where appropriate ❑ Software documentation
Client-side integration	❑ Deliver and assist with installation of server hardware ❑ Coordinate with interactive technologies department for installation onto local area network (LAN)	❑ Functional Web server on client LAN
Client-side testing	❑ Conduct friendly beta testing ❑ Publicly beta-test.process	❑ Consolidated list of actual and perceived bugs ❑ Action plan and budgets for bug resolution

Notes

Chapter 1

1. Bernhard Warner and Miguel Helft. "How Culture Clash Sank the Toys 'R' Us Deal," *The Standard: Intelligence for the Internet Economy*, August 20, 1999.

2. Clayton Christenson. *The Innovator's Dilemma.* Harvard Press, 1997.

3. Securities and Exchange Commission Statistics as of 8/1/99. Further data available at www.sec.gov.

4. Megan Barnett. "Merrill Talks, Brokers Walk," *The Standard: Intelligence for the Internet Economy*, October 11, 1999.

5. An elaboration on this theory can be found in Geoffrey Moore's book *Crossing the Chasm.*

Chapter 2

1. You can also access this worksheet electronically at www.focazio.com.

Chapter 3

1. Real Networks (www.real.com) offers a free product called "Real Jukebox" that will convert entire CDs into MP3 files.

Chapter 4

1. Sean Maloney, VP of Marketing, Intel Corporation.

2. *Time Warner Annual Report*, 1999.

Chapter 8

1. Quicken™ is a trademark of Intuit. Used for identification purposes only.

Chapter 9

1. *1999 Dell Annual Report* at <u>www.dell.com</u>.

Chapter 10

1. Denise Caruso, Business and Financial Section, *The New York Times*, February 28, 2000.

2. *Federal Express Annual Report*, 1997.

INDEX

continued